Jayne Netley Mayhew's
CROSS STITCH
Flowers

D&C
David and Charles

For my Ian
and Lorraine and Ian – lifelong friends

A DAVID & CHARLES BOOK
David & Charles is a subsidiary of F+W (UK) Ltd.,
an F+W Publications Inc. company

First published in the UK in 2005

Distributed in North America
by F+W Publications, Inc.
4700 East Galbraith Road
Cincinnati, OH 45236
1-800-289-0963

A catalogue record for this book is available from the British Library.

ISBN 0 7153 1585 4

Executive editor Cheryl Brown
Editor Jennifer Proverbs
Senior designer Lisa Forrester
Project editor Lin Clements
Styled photography Kim Sayer
Other photography Karl Adamson

Printed in Singapore by KHL
for David & Charles
Brunel House   Newton Abbot   Devon

Visit our website at www.davidandcharles.co.uk

David & Charles books are available from all good bookshops; alternatively
you can contact our Orderline on (0)1626 334555 or write to us at
FREEPOST EX2 110, David & Charles Direct, Newton Abbot, TQ12 4ZZ
(no stamp required UK mainland).

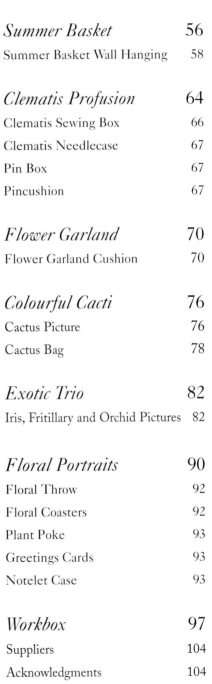

Contents

Introduction

This is my sixth book of cross stitch designs and I'm delighted to bring you a collection of one of your most popular subjects for stitching – the wonderful world of flowers. I had an amazing variety of flowers to choose from, wild and cultivated, tiny and statuesque, all with a beautiful array of colour and shape. My final selection ranges from pretty spring-flowering bulbs and hot summer blooms to delicate cornfield flowers and classic roses, so I am sure you will find many of your favourites here.

My floral designs feature on a wide range of lovely projects. There are attractive framed pictures and wall hangings, beautiful bed and table linen, a sumptuous quilt and cushions, pretty bath linen, a wooden sewing box and accessories and a Victorian-style footstool. Smaller, quick-stitch projects include cards, coasters, a scented bag, trinket pot and plant poke. My choice of flowers and projects will suit all levels of experience – from the absolute

beginner to the experienced stitcher who enjoys a challenge. A great many
of the designs are extremely versatile and I'm sure you will have fun devising
new ways to use them. To get you started there are suggestions throughout
for alternative ways to display the designs.

The projects have easy-to-follow colour charts and full stitching and
making up instructions. A useful Workbox section, which begins on page 97,
describes the equipment and materials you will need for cross stitching, the
basic stitching techniques required and some general making up methods.

Flowers are a perennially favourite subject for cross stitch, and no wonder
for they have it all – fabulous colours and fascinating shapes. I was totally
inspired and excited by all the blooms I have included and hope you will
be too. So come on into the flower garden with me and enjoy many happy
hours of stitching.

Perfect Peonies

Peonies, one of the glories of the flower border, have long been valued for their bold foliage and wonderfully showy blooms. They were once highly valued as a medicinal plant and were used by physicians to treat a wide range of ailments.

This lovely picture is charted in whole cross stitch but to add a three-dimensional, textured look you could use bullion knots for the centre stamens or French knots or even beads. The design is versatile, allowing you to stitch smaller motifs to decorate a range of items, such as a pretty trinket pot and card shown on pages 8 and 9.

Peony Picture

Stitch count 125 x 150

Design size 23 x 27cm (9 x 10¾in) approx

You Will Need

Cream 28-count Zweigart Cashel linen
40 x 47cm (15¾ x 18½in)

DMC stranded cotton (floss) as listed in chart
key (1 skein of each colour)

Tapestry needle size 24–26

1 Prepare your fabric for work and mark the
centre point (see page 98). Work outwards
from the centre of the chart on pages 10–11.

2 Work over two threads of linen, using two
strands of stranded cotton (floss) for all
cross stitch. Although the chart is shown as
cross stitch, you could stitch the centre sections
of the flowers (colours 744, 743, 742 and 741)
with bullion knots instead (instructions on
page 100). Use two strands of thread and work
from the centres outwards, filling them with a
mixture of bullion knots in varying lengths, as
shown in the detail picture below.

3 Once all the stitching is complete, mount
and frame your picture (see page 102 for
advice on framing).

Trinket Pot

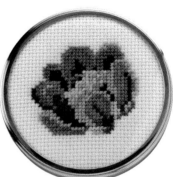

Stitch count 26 x 30

Design size 4 x 4.75cm (1½ x 1¾in)

Using the main chart, stitch one of the
smaller peony flowers (top left) to create a lovely
trinket pot – the one shown here is a 7.5cm (3in) diameter pot from
Framecraft, see Suppliers. Use a 15cm (6in) square of cream 16-count
Aida and work in cross stitch over one block using two strands of thread.
Follow the manufacturer's instructions for mounting the finished
stitching into the pot lid.

Peony Card

Stitch count 56 x 34

Design size 10 x 6cm (4 x 2½in)

This pretty card (shown right) also uses the main chart and features the
bottom-right peony flower with some leaves as well. Use a 21 x 26cm
(8 x 10in) piece of cream 14-count Aida and work over one block. Use
two strands of thread for the cross stitch and work French knots instead
of cross stitch for colours 744, 743, 742 and 741 in the flower centres.
I've used a cream card with a 9.5 x 13.5cm (3¾ x 5⅛in) oblong aperture
(Framecraft, see Suppliers). See page 102 for making up into a card.

Perfect Peonies
DMC stranded cotton
Cross stitch

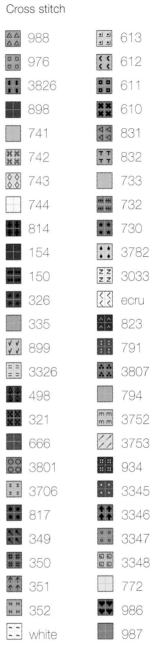

988		613	
976		612	
3826		611	
898		610	
741		831	
742		832	
743		733	
744		732	
814		730	
154		3782	
150		3033	
326		ecru	
335		823	
899		791	
3326		3807	
498		794	
321		3752	
666		3753	
3801		934	
3706		3345	
817		3346	
349		3347	
350		3348	
351		772	
352		986	
white		987	

Wild Flower Borders

I have selected some of my favourite wild flowers to create violet, periwinkle, buttercup and primrose designs. The sweet violet inspired four borders stitched on Aida band and waste canvas to adorn bed linen and a scent bag. Violets have long been the scent of love and the petal oil is still used in toiletries and flavourings. Periwinkles, buttercups and primroses were once used by herbalists to treat a variety of ailments but you can use them to bring an extra special look to towels and face cloths.

All of the designs are versatile and easy to stitch, using full and three-quarter cross stitch, backstitch and French knots. Refer to charts for stitch counts and design sizes.

Violet Bed Linen

Turn a simple sheet and pillowcase into something special by stitching on violet-strewn Aida bands. You could also use the designs to edge bathrobe pockets, towels and tea towels.

You Will Need

For the sheet: white Aida band, 5cm (2in) wide x sheet width, plus turning allowance

For the pillowcase: white Aida band 9cm (3½in) x pillowcase width, plus turning allowance

For the pillowcase: four pieces of waste canvas 8 x 8cm (3 x 3in)

DMC stranded cotton (floss) as listed in chart key (1 skein of each colour)

Tapestry needle size 24–26

Matching sewing thread

Stitching the sheet band

1 Mark the centre of the band and begin stitching 6mm (¼in) from one end. Follow Violet A chart on page 16, repeating the design to the desired length. Use two strands of stranded cotton (floss) for cross stitch, one strand of 3346 for backstitch and one of 310 for French knots.

2 When the embroidery is complete, turn the ends of the band under by 6mm (¼in) and then pin, tack (baste) and machine stitch the band on to the sheet.

Stitching the pillowcase band

Follow the instructions for the sheet but use Violet B chart. If you wish, you could add a ribbon in a matching colour along the edge of the design to finish.

Stitching the Oxford pillowcase

Work Violets C and D on the corners using waste canvas (see page 99), and following step 2 above. Edge the pillowcase with a 6mm wide mauve ribbon, overlapping the corners, as shown here.

Scent Bag

I have used a mixture of violet designs on this bag but one sprig and a border of flower heads would look just as lovely.

You Will Need

Pearl fleck 14-count Aida (Zweigart code 11) 31 x 31cm (12 x 12in)

DMC stranded cotton (floss) as listed in chart key (1 skein of each colour)

Tapestry needle size 24–26

Matching ribbon 6mm (¼in) wide x 30cm (12in) long

Scrap of lace for edging (optional)

Matching sewing thread

Violet-scented pot-pourri

1 Fold the fabric in half and mark the centre line. Draw or tack (baste) a square guideline on the fabric about 20 x 24cm (7¾ x 9½in), ensuring it is placed evenly on the centre line. Mark the centre point of each half, allowing for 6mm (¼in) turnings on the edges.

2 Follow the stitching instructions in step 2 of the sheet band, left, but use a mixture of the individual Violet E designs on page 16. Allow a gap between the designs for the ribbon tie.

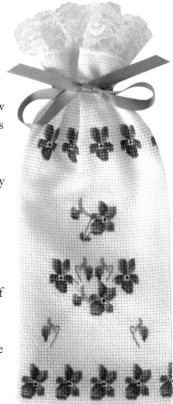

3 When the embroidery is complete, trim off any excess fabric. Hem the top edge then pin, tack (baste) and machine stitch along the side and bottom. Stitch a length of lace to the hemmed top edge. Fill the bag with scented pot-pourri and tie the piece of ribbon in a bow around the neck of the bag to finish.

Wild Flower Bath Linen

Wild flowers make charming cross stitch motifs and periwinkles, buttercups and primroses stitched on Aida bands are the perfect decoration for towels and face cloths.

You Will Need

For the towels: white Aida bands 9cm (3½in) wide and 5.5cm (2½in) wide x the towel width, plus turning allowance

For the face cloth: white Aida band 5.5cm (2½in) wide x face cloth width, plus turning allowance

DMC stranded cotton (floss) as listed in chart key (1 skein of each colour)

Tapestry needle size 24–26

Matching sewing thread

Stitching the towel band

1 Mark the centre of the Aida band and begin stitching 6mm (¼in) from one end of the Aida band, to leave enough for a turning.

2 Use two strands of stranded cotton (floss) for cross stitch and one strand of 988 for backstitch. Follow the chart of your choice on page 17, repeating the design from left to right to the desired length. When stitching the large periwinkle, stitch the polka dots to fill the height and depth of the Aida band.

3 When the embroidery is complete, turn the ends of the band under by 6mm (¼in) and then pin, tack (baste) and machine stitch the band on to the towel.

Stitching the face cloth band

Follow the instructions for the towel band, using the chart of your choice on page 17.

Bring the wild flower garden into your home with these charming designs. They can be used in many ways: stitch a flower head on a small fabric count for buttons or change the colours completely to create something new.

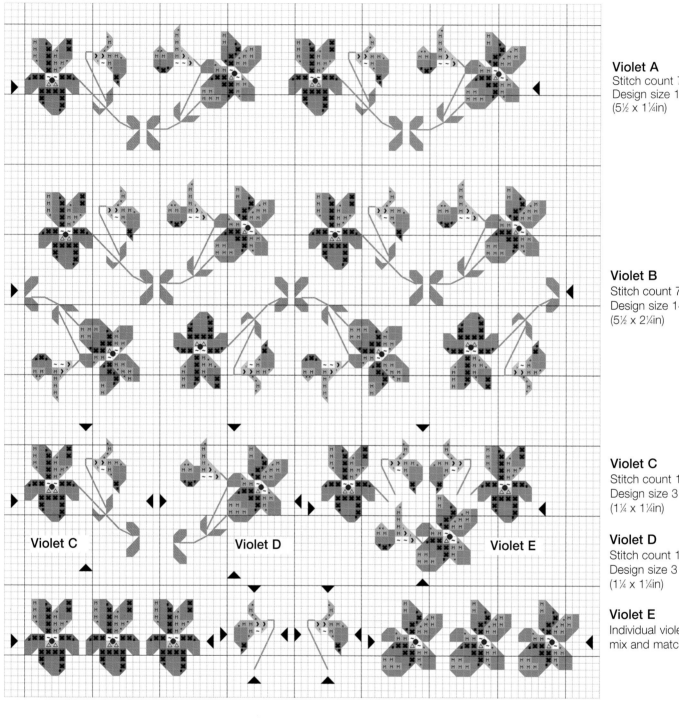

Violet A
Stitch count 74 x 18
Design size 14 x 3cm
(5½ x 1¼in)

Violet B
Stitch count 79 x 32
Design size 14 x 6cm
(5½ x 2¼in)

Violet C
Stitch count 17 x 17
Design size 3 x 3cm
(1¼ x 1¼in)

Violet D
Stitch count 17 x 18
Design size 3 x 3cm
(1¼ x 1¼in)

Violet E
Individual violets for
mix and match

Violets
DMC stranded cotton
Cross stitch

white	333	340	3348
310	743	3746	3346

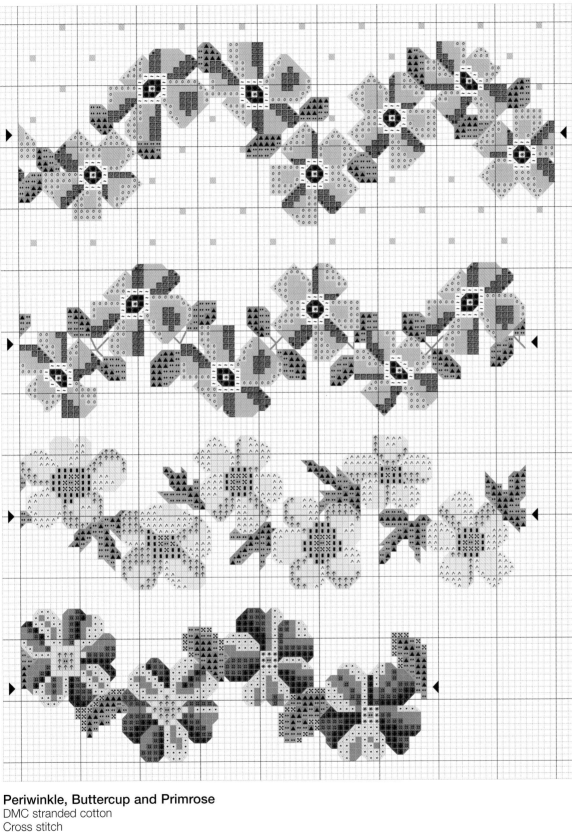

Large Periwinkle
Stitch count 90 x 36
Design size 16 x 6cm
(6½ x 2½in)

Small Periwinkle
Stitch count 85 x 25
Design size 15 x 5cm
(6 x 2in)

Buttercup
Stitch count 85 x 25
Design size 15 x 5cm
(6 x 2in)

Primrose
Stitch count 85 x 25
Design size 15 x 5cm
(6 x 2in)

Periwinkle, Buttercup and Primrose
DMC stranded cotton
Cross stitch

151	3731	472	727	742	988	211	209	white
3733	3350	3078	726	989	745	210	327	

Victorian Bouquet

The design in this chapter was inspired by a
very old Victorian footstool. It was originally
stitched by the grandmother of the family
and has become an heirloom, so well used
through the years that it is now a little worn
and faded. I have recreated the design here,
with a little of my own inspiration along the
way, using a mixture of wool (yarn), stranded
cotton (floss) and beads – a combination
that creates a delightful effect.
Using the same chart but working in cross
stitch on a sage-green Aida with stranded
cottons, you could also create the lovely
frilled cushion shown on page 21.

Victorian Footstool

The footstool as shown uses an interesting mixture of wool (yarn), stranded cotton (floss) and beads but you could use just wool throughout if you prefer.

Stitch count 163 x 161

Design size 30 x 29cm (11⅝ x 11½in) approx

You Will Need

14-count interlock tapestry canvas
56 x 56cm (22 x 22in)

DMC D475 Broder Medicis wool (yarn) as listed in chart key (1 skein of each colour)

DMC D478 Broder Medicis wool (yarn),
1 hank of black

Optional DMC stranded cotton (floss):
1 skein 676; 2 skeins 951

Optional DMC seed beads: 1 pack each grey,
black-brown and topaz; 3 packs of copper

Tapestry needle size 24–26 and a beading needle

Footstool 33cm (13in) square
(Market Square, see Suppliers)

1 Prepare your canvas for work and mark the centre (see page 98). Work outwards from the centre of the chart on pages 22–25.

2 If working the stool only in wool (yarn), work in cross stitch over one thread of canvas using two strands throughout. Continue stitching the black background until you reach the desired size of the footstool.

If working the stool in a mixture of wool (yarn), stranded cotton (floss) and beads (see details, right), replace the wool with six strands of stranded cotton as follows: wool 8314 with cotton 676, and ecru wool with cotton 951. Replace wool colours 8507, 8500, 8325 and 8176 with the same colour beads. See page 99 for attaching beads.

3 Once all stitching is complete, check for missed stitches and mount in the footstool according to the manufacturer's instructions.

Replacing areas of cross stitch with beads is very simple to do and can create the most wonderful effects, bringing additional sparkle and three-dimensional texture to even the simplest design. See page 99 for guidance when attaching beads.

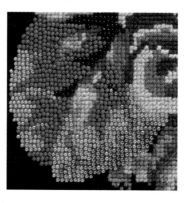

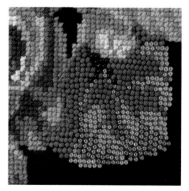

Victorian Cushion

The cushion uses the same chart as the footstool but is worked only in stranded cotton (floss) on Aida, which means the background does not need to be stitched.

Stitch count 163 x 161

Design size 30 x 29cm (11⅝ x 11½in) approx

You Will Need

Sage green 14-count Aida 56 x 56cm (22 x 22in)

DMC stranded cotton (floss) as listed in chart key (1 skein of each colour)

Tapestry needle size 24–26

Fabric for backing and frill 1m (1yd) approx

Cushion pad 38 x 38cm (15 x 15in)

Matching sewing thread

1 Prepare your fabric for work and mark the centre point (see page 98). Work outwards from the centre of the chart on pages 22–25.

2 Work over one block of Aida, using two strands of stranded cotton (floss) for all cross stitch. Do not stitch the black background for the cushion.

3 Once all the stitching is complete, check for missed stitches and then make up into a frilled cushion following the instructions in Workbox, page 102.

top left

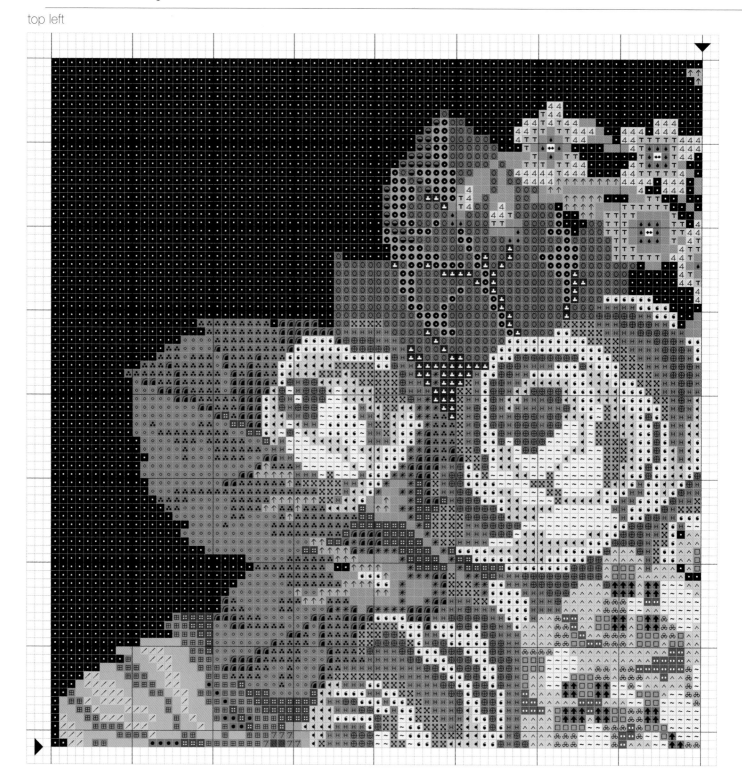

Victorian Bouquet

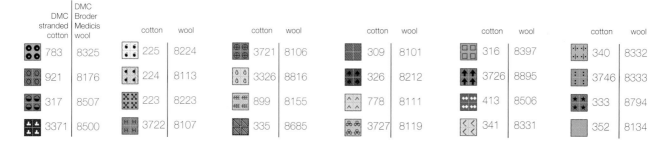

DMC stranded cotton	DMC Broder Medicis wool	cotton	wool	cotton	wool	cotton	wool	cotton	wool	cotton	wool
783	8325	225	8224	3721	8106	309	8101	316	8397	340	8332
921	8176	224	8113	3326	8816	326	8212	3726	8895	3746	8333
317	8507	223	8223	899	8155	778	8111	413	8506	333	8794
3371	8500	3722	8107	335	8685	3727	8119	341	8331	352	8134

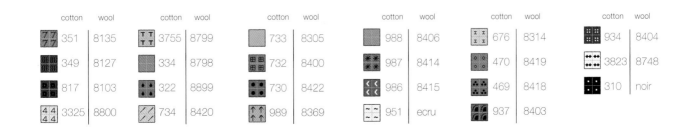

	cotton	wool		cotton	wool		cotton	wool		cotton	wool		cotton	wool		cotton	wool
	351	8135		3755	8799		733	8305		988	8406		676	8314		934	8404
	349	8127		334	8798		732	8400		987	8414		470	8419		3823	8748
	817	8103		322	8899		730	8422		986	8415		469	8418		310	noir
	3325	8800		734	8420		989	8369		951	ecru		937	8403			

bottom left

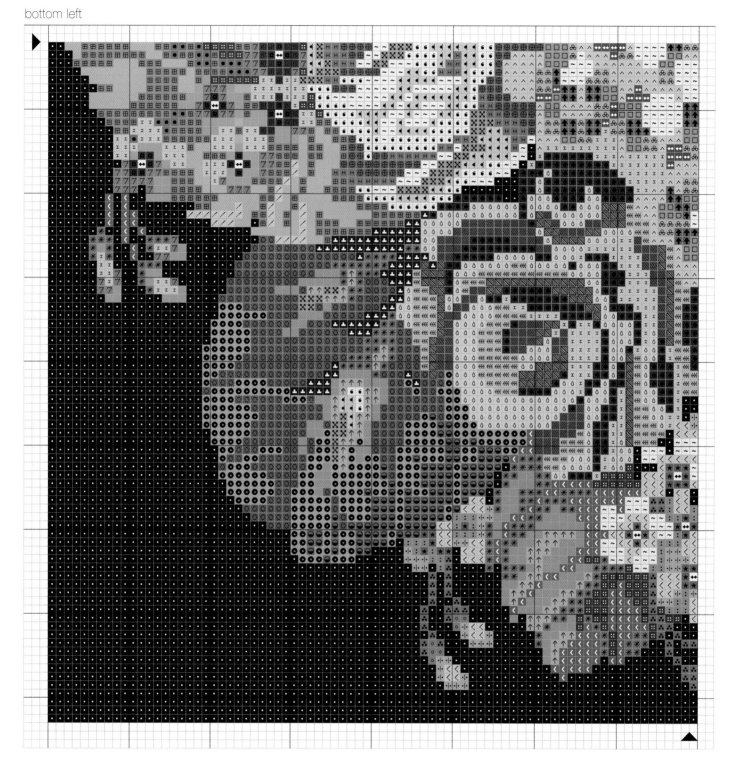

Victorian Bouquet

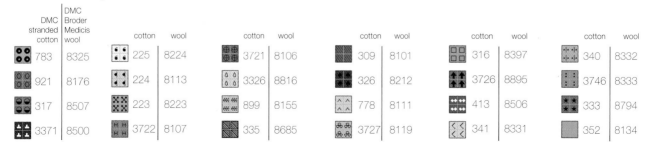

	DMC stranded cotton	DMC Broder Medicis wool		cotton	wool		cotton	wool		cotton	wool		cotton	wool		cotton	wool
	783	8325		225	8224		3721	8106		309	8101		316	8397		340	8332
	921	8176		224	8113		3326	8816		326	8212		3726	8895		3746	8333
	317	8507		223	8223		899	8155		778	8111		413	8506		333	8794
	3371	8500		3722	8107		335	8685		3727	8119		341	8331		352	8134

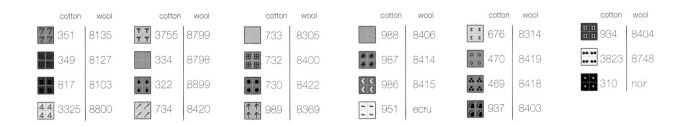

	cotton	wool		cotton	wool		cotton	wool		cotton	wool		cotton	wool		cotton	wool
	351	8135		3755	8799		733	8305		988	8406		676	8314		934	8404
	349	8127		334	8798		732	8400		987	8414		470	8419		3823	8748
	817	8103		322	8899		730	8422		986	8415		469	8418		310	noir
	3325	8800		734	8420		989	8369		951	ecru		937	8403			

Spring Flowers

The delicate but hardy snowdrop, bluebell, daffodil and fritillary are a must for any spring garden and a sure sign that winter is coming to an end. I have shown them here stitched as a dramatic wall hanging on black Aida – a wonderful focal point for any room. If you prefer, you could create a set of lovely pictures by stitching the flowers individually, with or without borders, as shown on page 29.

Wall Hanging

Stitch count 221 x 181

Design size 40 x 33cm (15¾ x 13in) approx

Finished size of wall hanging

56 x 47cm (22 x 18½in)

You Will Need

Black 14-count Aida 54 x 61cm (21 x 24in)

DMC stranded cotton (floss) as listed in chart key (1 skein of each colour and 2 skeins of 733)

Tapestry needle size 24–26

Cream fabric for border and backing, two pieces 60 x 50cm (24 x 20in) approx

Wadding (batting) 56 x 47cm (22 x 18½in)

Matching sewing thread

Four brass or wooden rings

Wooden dowel, 1.25cm (½in) diameter x 60cm (24in) long

1 Prepare your fabric for work and mark the centre point (see page 98). The wall hanging uses all four designs charted on pages 30–33, with a space of one stitch between the borders of each design.

2 Work outwards from the centre of the four-chart design. Stitch over one block of Aida, using two strands of stranded cotton (floss) for all full and three-quarter cross stitch. Work backstitch with one strand of 369 for the snowdrop flower stems, 792 for bluebell flower details and 986 for fritillary flower stems. Work backstitch with two strands of 320 for snowdrops stems and 733 for all borders.

3 Once all stitching is complete, make up as a wall hanging as follows. Trim the embroidered fabric down to the desired size, centre it on the border fabric piece and pin, tack (baste) and stitch in place all around the edges of the embroidery (see Fig 1). If you want to fray the edges of the Aida, move the stitching line (shown by the dashed line) inwards 2cm (³⁄₄in). Create a neat edge by double folding the edges of the cream fabric over to the front side and carefully pinning, tacking (basting) and stitching it in place.

Fig 1 Stitching the embroidery centrally to the border fabric.

4 Lay the wadding (batting) centrally on to the piece of backing fabric. Fold the edges of the fabric in, over the wadding, to the same size as the front. Pin, tack (baste) and stitch in place, so the wadding edges are enclosed and held in place. Put the front and back together, creating a 'sandwich' as indicated in Fig 2, and slipstitch together all around the edges. Remove the tacking.

5 Fray the edges of the Aida all round and add other decoration of your choice – I have stitched on two borders of thin gold braid. Sew the four brass or wooden rings along the back of the hanging and insert the wooden dowel for hanging.

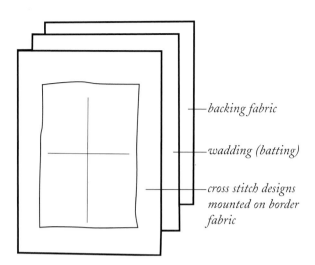

— *backing fabric*

— *wadding (batting)*

— *cross stitch designs mounted on border fabric*

Fig 2 Padding and backing the embroidery.

Spring Flower Pictures

Stitch count 110 x 90 with border; 83 x 62 without border

Design size 20 x 16.5cm (7¾ x 6½in) with border; 15 x 11cm (6 x 4⅓in) without border

Stitch the pretty spring flowers as individual framed pictures using the charts on pages 30–33. For each flower use a 38 x 33cm (15 x 13in) piece of natural 14-count Aida and follow the stitching instructions in step 2 of the wall hanging on page 26. Mount and frame as a picture to finish (see page 102).

Snowdrop
DMC stranded
cotton
Cross stitch

↑↑/↑↑	369
✳✳/✳✳	368
✚✚/✚✚	320
♥♥/♥♥	367
HH/HH	928
OO/OO	927
•• /••	926
▨	733
⁻⁻/⁻⁻	white

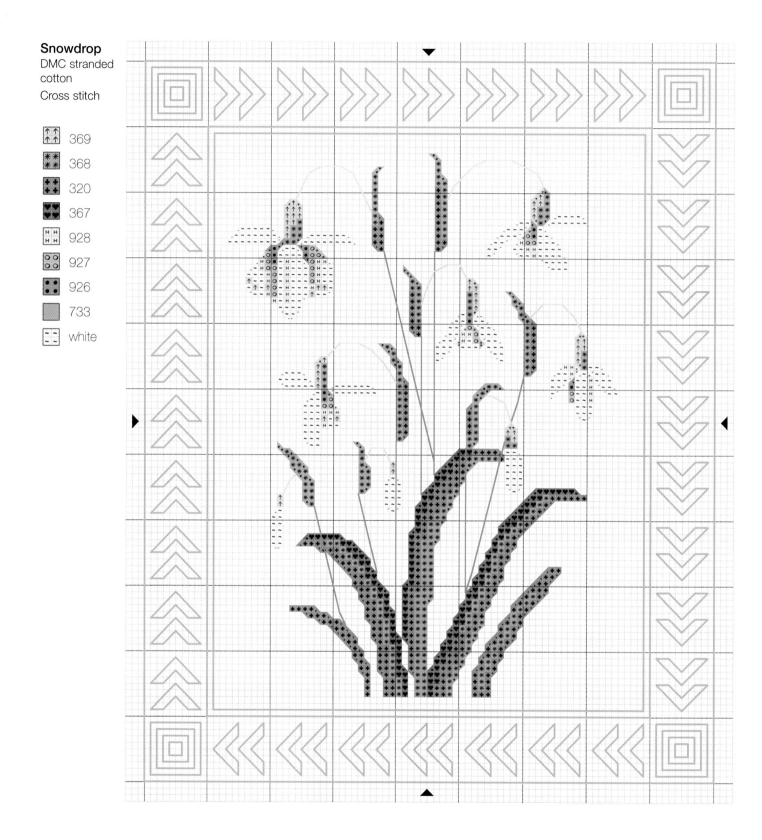

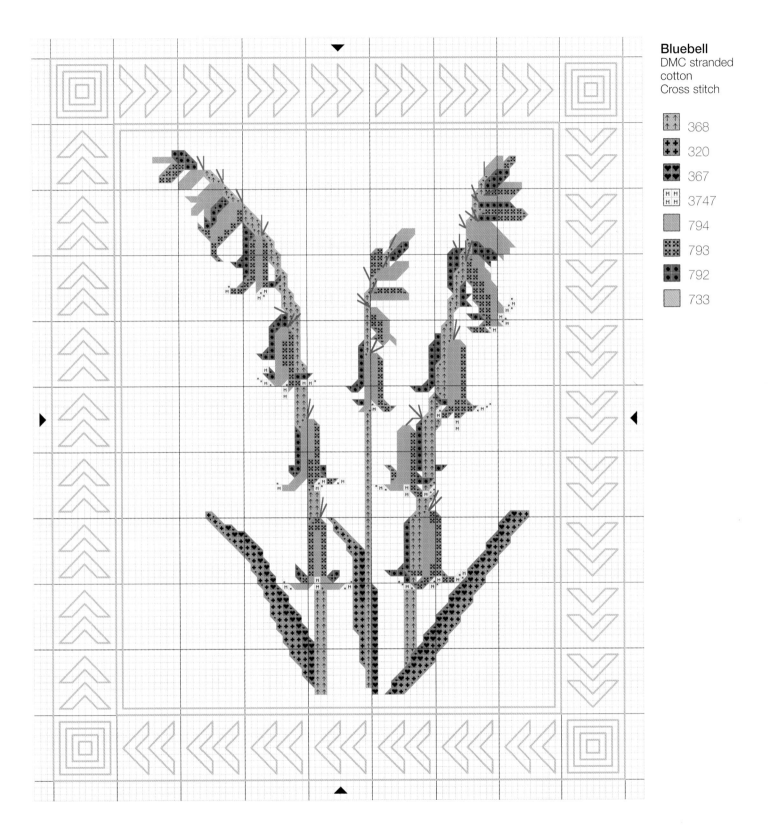

Bluebell
DMC stranded
cotton
Cross stitch

↑↑ ↑↑	368
✚✚ ✚✚	320
♥♥ ♥♥	367
H H H H	3747
▦	794
▦	793
•• ••	792
▨	733

Fritillary
DMC stranded
cotton
Cross stitch

↑↑ ↑↑	988
✚✚ ✚✚	987
♥♥ ♥♥	986
H H H H	3689
◣◥ ◥◣	3688
▨	3687
▦	3803
✚✚ ✚✚	902
▥	733

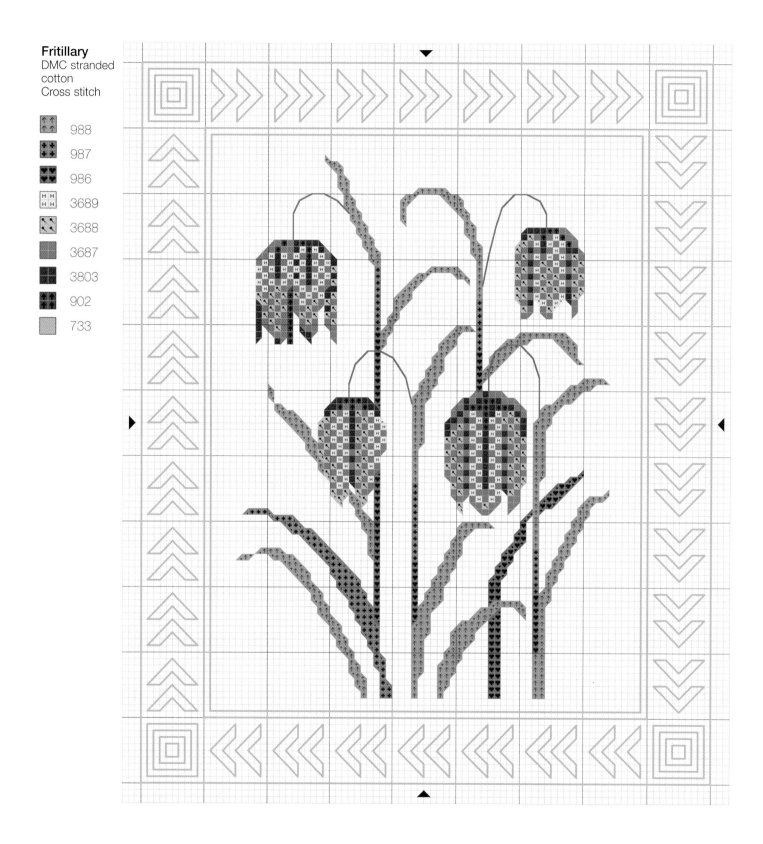

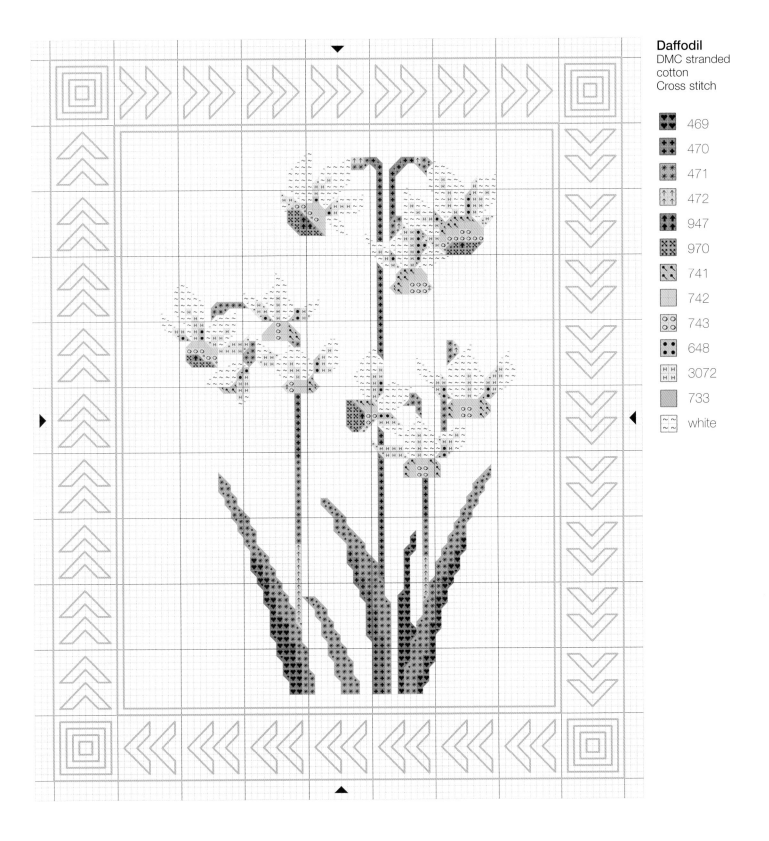

Daffodil
DMC stranded
cotton
Cross stitch

♥♥	469
✚✚	470
✳✳	471
↑↑	472
↟↟	947
✖✖	970
◥◢	741
	742
◔◔	743
••	648
H H	3072
	733
~ ~	white

Fuchsias and Lilies

Fuchsias and lilies are two of the most beautiful flowers. Some say fuchsias are like jewels hung on branches; for me they are like dancers – some tiny and refined, others big, colourful and blowsy. Lilies also come in many shapes and colours; some are so beautiful they hardly look real, and most have a delicious scent.

I have used these two flowers to create border designs which are ideal for decorating many items. They are shown here stitched on Aida band for towels and on small pieces of Aida for face cloths, but they could also be used on brightly coloured tea towels, as shown on page 36.

Fuchsia and Lily Bath Linen

Stitch counts

Fuchsia 28 x 80

Lily 40 x 90

Design sizes

Fuchsia 5 x 14.5cm (2 x 5¾in)

Lily 7.5 x 16.5cm (2¾ x 6½in)

You Will Need

For the fuchsia towel: white Aida band 7cm (2½in) wide x towel width, plus turning allowance

For the lily towel: white Aida band 9cm (3½in) wide x face cloth width, plus turning allowance

For the face cloth: 15 x 15cm (6 x 6in) white 14-count Aida

DMC stranded cotton (floss) as listed in chart keys (1 skein of each colour)

Tapestry needle size 24–26

Matching sewing thread

Stitching the towel band

1 Mark the centre of the Aida band and begin stitching 6mm (¼in) from one end, to leave enough for a turning. Follow the chart opposite, using the wide band for the lily and the narrower band for the fuchsia, repeating the design from left to right to the desired length.

2 Use two strands of stranded cotton (floss) for all cross stitch. Work backstitch using one strand of 320 for the fuchsia flower stems, 150 for fuchsia stamens, 721 around the lily petals and 919 for lily details.

3 When the embroidery is complete, turn the ends of the band under by 6mm (¼in) and then pin, tack (baste) and machine stitch the band on to the towel.

Tea Towels

Why not stitch the lily and fuchsia borders to decorate tea towels and bring a pretty, summery look to your kitchen? Use Aida band as before and follow the instructions, left.

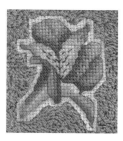

Stitching the face cloth

Stitch a single lily flower on white Aida, following the stitching instructions in step 2 above. When complete, trim off excess fabric leaving one stitch width all around the design. Attach to the face cloth by machine stitching around the edges.

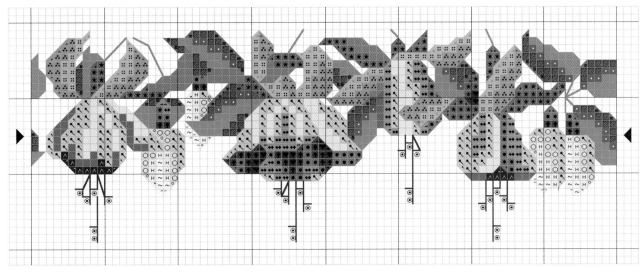

Fuchsia
DMC stranded cotton
Cross stitch

3354		894		3834		
151		150		3835		367
761		3350		891		320
3713		3731		892		3823
3770		3733		893		319

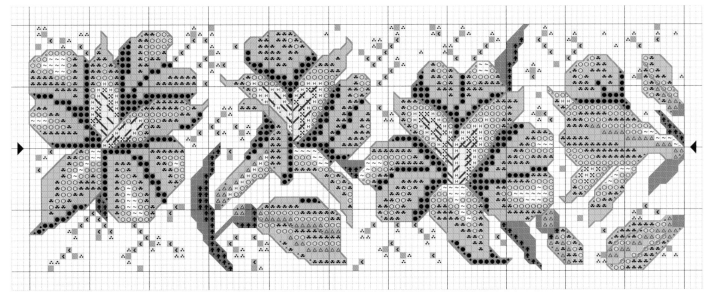

Lily
DMC stranded cotton
Cross stitch

721		3347		563	
741		3348		3747	
742		744		340	
743		745		919	
white		3823		3346	

Patchwork Roses

Roses have been favourites for hundreds of years, and today are grown

in a gorgeous range of colours and shapes – a rose to suit every taste.

Most have a heavenly scent too and, understandably, are associated with love.

Here I have created a romantic patchwork quilt and cushions with four

rose designs. For quick projects why not stitch a single rose for a card, trinket pot,

pincushion or little picture?

Rose Quilt

You Will Need

White 14-count Aida 1.4m x 110cm (1½yd x 40in)

DMC stranded cotton (floss) as listed in chart key (1 skein each white, 3721, 772, 890; 2 skeins each 3326, 335, 776, 818, 899, 221, 223, 225, 3345, 3346, 3348, 3722, 895; 3 skeins each 309, 224, 3347; 4 skeins of 819)

Tapestry needle size 24–26

Three different fabrics for the patchwork:
fabric a (for patchwork squares)
50 x 115cm (⅝yd x 45in) wide

fabric b (for patchwork squares and outer border)
1.5m x 115cm (1⅝yd x 45in) wide

fabric c (for inner border and edging)
1.5m x 115cm (1⅝yd x 45in) wide

Backing fabric 3.10m x 90cm (3⅜yd x 36in) wide

Lightweight polyester wadding (batting)
3.10m x 90cm (3⅜yd x 36in) wide

Matching sewing thread and quilting thread (optional)

The quilt features all four rose designs in a patchwork with three cotton fabrics. The centre panel is made first, with borders added to an overall size of 152cm (60in) square. Refer to charts for stitch counts and design sizes.

Stitching the embroidered squares

You will need seventeen embroidered squares – six Rose A, six Rose B, two Rose C and three Rose D (polka dots optional).

1 Use a pencil to mark out seventeen 27cm (10¾in) squares on the Aida. Follow the charts on pages 42–45 and work each design from the centre outwards, using two strands of stranded cotton (floss) for all cross stitch. Work backstitch with one strand of 309 for Rose A and C and 221 for Rose B and D. If stitching the polka dots in Rose C and D, work the pattern to the edges of the square. When the embroidered squares are complete, cut away excess fabric so each measures 21cm (8¼in) square, making sure the rose design is central on each.

Stitching the centre panel

The centre panel is made up from thirteen embroidered squares and twelve patchwork squares. Each patchwork square is created from nine smaller squares of fabrics a and b (see the layout in Fig 1 overleaf) to create a finished size of 21cm (8¼in) square.

2 To make the nine-patch squares, cut a 9cm (3½in) square template from thick card. With the fabric right side down on a flat surface, use a pencil to draw around the template to mark out the squares. Cut sixty squares from fabric a, and forty-eight squares from fabric b. Be accurate when marking and cutting so the patchwork squares will fit correctly when sewn together. Seam allowances are included.

3 Arrange the nine fabric pieces for each nine-patch square as shown in Fig 1, below. Each nine-patch is assembled from three strips of three squares each. To make each strip, pin the squares together, right sides facing and fabric edges matching. Pin and machine stitch 1.5cm (⅝in) from this edge. Press seams open. Repeat this process until you have completed all twelve squares.

4 Arrange the twelve patchwork squares and the thirteen embroidered squares in the order shown in Fig 1. Stitch the centre panel together in the same way as you did for the patchwork squares, with the same seam allowances, but this time with five strips of five squares each. When all five strips are joined together, press the seams.

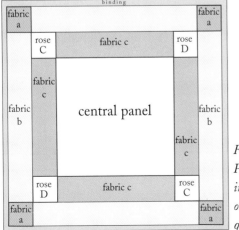

Fig 1 Central patchwork panel.

Stitching the borders

5 Make the inner border by cutting four strips from fabric c, each 93 x 21cm (36¼ x 8¼in). With right sides facing, pin, tack (baste) and stitch one strip to the top of the panel and one to the bottom (see Fig 2). Press seams.

Take the two remaining border strips and, with the right sides facing, pin, tack (baste) and stitch an embroidered square to each short edge. Press seams. With right sides facing, pin, tack (baste) and stitch a strip to each side of the central panel. Press seams.

6 Make the outer border by cutting four strips from fabric b, each 129 x 15.5cm (50¼ x 6⅛in), and four squares from fabric a, each 15.5cm (6⅛in) square. Join to the quilt in the same way as the inner border but replacing the embroidered squares with the squares cut from fabric a (see Fig 2).

Backing, quilting and binding

7 Cut two pieces of backing fabric each 154 x 78.5cm (61 x 30⅝in). With right sides facing, pin, tack (baste) and stitch the long edges together using a 1.5cm (⅝in) seam allowance as before and so the seam line runs down the centre of the backing fabric. Press seams open.

8 Cut two pieces of wadding (batting) each 154cm (31in) long. Join the two lengths into one large piece by butting the long edges together with herringbone stitch or long tacking (basting) stitches on both sides. Lay the backing fabric right side down on a flat surface, lay the wadding (batting) on top and the patchwork on top of this, right side up. Pin this 'quilt sandwich' together from the centre outwards. Tack (baste) all three layers together in a grid pattern.

9 Quilt the patchwork by hand or machine, using a simple running stitch with either sewing or quilting thread. The easiest way of doing this is to stitch along the patchwork square seam lines to give each piece more definition and to secure the wadding (batting). Remove the tacking (basting) when all quilting is finished.

10 To finish the quilt, bind the raw outer edges using enough 7cm (2¾in) wide strips of fabric c to fit all around. Stitch the strips together to form one long strip. Press a 1.5cm (⅝in) hem along each long edge and then press the strip in half, so the hemmed edges are enclosed. With right sides facing, lay the binding on the right side of the quilt so the first pressed hem is 2cm (¾in) from the outside edges. Pin, tack (baste) and stitch in place, mitring the corners (Fig 3). Turn the border strip over to the back of the quilt to form an edging, hand stitching it in place.

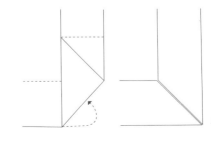

Fig 3 Mitring corners.

Fig 2 Placement of the inner border, outer border and quilt binding.

Rose Cushions

These charming patchwork cushions feature rose designs A and C but any of the four designs could be used. Each cushion is made up in stages, starting with a centre embroidered square, with two contrasting fabric borders then added. The overall cushion size, excluding frill is 38cm (15in) square. Refer to the charts for the stitch counts and design sizes.

You Will Need (to make both cushions)

Two pieces of white 11-count Aida 31 x 31cm (12 x 12in)

DMC stranded cotton (floss) as listed in chart key
(1 skein of each colour)

Tapestry needle size 24–26

Two different fabrics for the patchwork
(sufficient for backing and frill too):
    fabric a 1m x 115cm (39 x 45in) wide
    fabric b 1m x 115cm (39 x 45in) wide

Matching sewing thread

Cushion pad 38 x 38cm (15 x 15in)

1 To make one cushion, first use a pencil to mark out a 25cm (9³⁄₄in) square on the Aida fabric. Follow the charts on pages 42–45, working the design of your choice from the centre outwards and using three strands of stranded cotton (floss) for all cross stitch. Work the backstitch with one strand of 309 for Rose A and C and 221 for Rose B and D. If stitching the polka dots in Rose C and D, continuing working the pattern until you reach the finished size of 21cm (8¹⁄₄in).

When the square is complete, cut away excess fabric so it measures 25cm (9³⁄₄in) square, making sure the rose design is central.

2 Create the patchwork as follows: from fabric a, cut two strips 25 x 7cm (9³⁄₄ x 2³⁄₄in) long and two 32.5 x 7cm (12³⁄₄ x 2³⁄₄in) long; from fabric b, cut two strips 32.5 x 7cm (12³⁄₄ x 2³⁄₄in) long and two strips 40 x 7cm (15³⁄₄ x 2³⁄₄in) long.

Take the embroidered square and one of the shorter lengths of fabric a. Pin the pieces together with right sides facing, matching edges, then machine stitch 1.5cm (⁵⁄₈in) from this edge. Press the seams. Repeat with the other short strip of fabric a on the opposite edge of the embroidered square (see layout in diagram, right). Take the embroidered patch and pin together with one of the longer strips of fabric a, right sides facing and edges matching. Machine stitch 1.5cm (⁵⁄₈in) from this edge. Do the same with the last length of fabric a on the other side to complete the border all round. Press the seams. Add an outer border with the four strips of fabric b in the same way. You can add as many borders as you wish until you reach the desired size for the finished cushion, remembering to increase the length of each strip each time.

3 Make the patchwork up into a cushion following the instructions in Workbox, page 102, using fabric a for the frill and backing. Reverse the border fabrics and frill when making the other cushion.

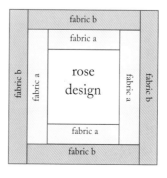

Patchwork layout for a cushion (reverse the border fabrics for the other cushion).

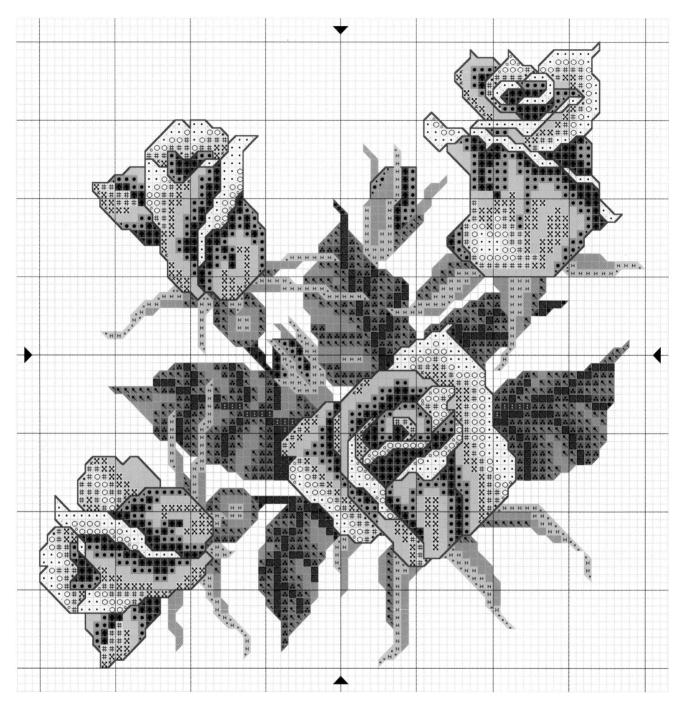

Rose A

DMC stranded cotton
Cross stitch

Stitch count 80 x 80
Design size (on 14-count): 14.5 x 14.5cm (5¾ x 5¾in)

890	3347	776	309
895	3348	3326	
3345	819	899	
3346	818	335	

Rose B
DMC stranded cotton
Cross stitch

Stitch count 77 x 75
Design size (on 14-count): 14 x 13.5cm (5½ x 5¼in)

■ 890	▨ 3347	◯◯ 225	● 3721			
■ 895	H H 3348	# # 224	▲ 221			
■ 3345	✓✓ 772	✕ 223	~ white			
■ 3346	∴ 819	■ 3722				

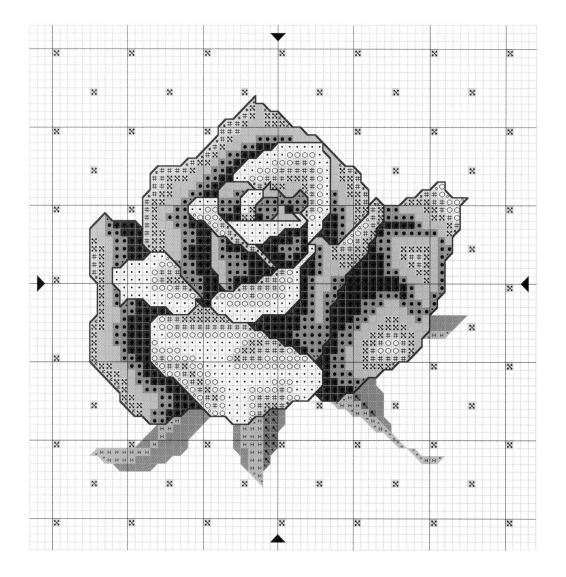

Rose C
DMC stranded cotton
Cross stitch

Stitch count 50 x 50 excluding polka dots
Design size (on 14-count): 9 x 9cm (3½ x 3½in)

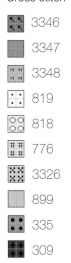

⬛	3346
⬛	3347
H H	3348
· ·	819
○○	818
# #	776
✕✕	3326
⬜	899
••	335
⬛	309

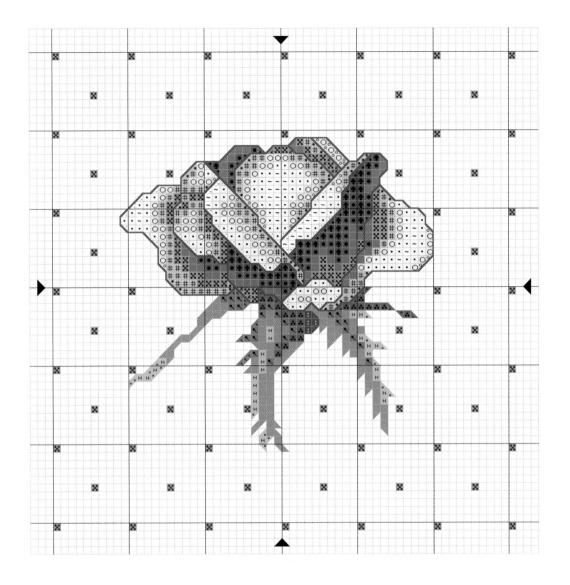

Rose D
DMC stranded cotton
Cross stitch

Stitch count 40 x 41 excluding polka dots
Design size (on 14-count): 7.5 x 7.5cm (3 x 3in)

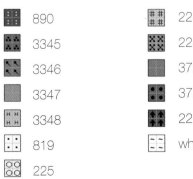

890	224
3345	223
3346	3722
3347	3721
3348	221
819	white
225	

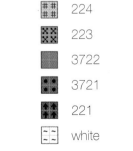

Cornfield Flowers

The warm colours of a ripening cornfield, with a flash of hot reds and mellow yellows, bring to mind the lazy days of summer on this table linen set. Poppies, corn, ox-eye daisies, black mustard, seed heads and grasses make up the tablecloth design, with three smaller motifs perfect for napkins. These cornfield flowers, worked in whole and three-quarter cross stitch, backstitch and French knots, could also be used on cards, trinket pots and plant pokes. The large design would make a wonderful cushion, stitched singly or in opposite corners. Refer to the charts for the stitch counts and design sizes for the various motifs.

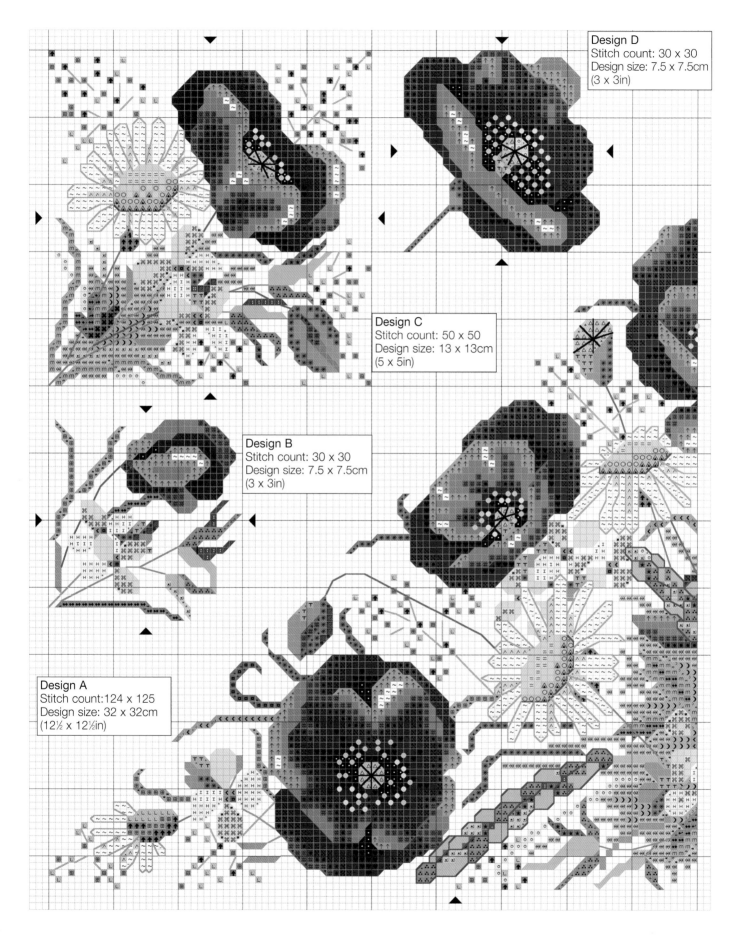

Design D
Stitch count: 30 x 30
Design size: 7.5 x 7.5cm
(3 x 3in)

Design C
Stitch count: 50 x 50
Design size: 13 x 13cm
(5 x 5in)

Design B
Stitch count: 30 x 30
Design size: 7.5 x 7.5cm
(3 x 3in)

Design A
Stitch count:124 x 125
Design size: 32 x 32cm
(12½ x 12½in)

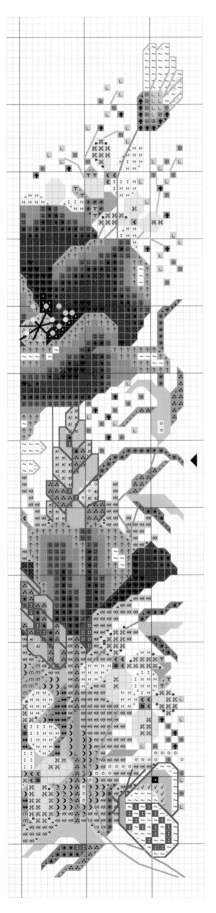

Cornfield Flowers
DMC stranded cotton
Cross stitch

V V	742	H H	3078
	741	I I	746
△ △	3046	○ ○	677
m m	471	⋈ ⋈	676
◆◆	470		422
✕ ✕	469	∴ ∴	3828
	642	★ ★	420
∧ ∧	644	⋮ ⋮	869
≪ ≪	613	▲ ▲	3852
⟩ ⟩	612	○○	3820
	935		3821
	986	≡ ≡	3822
✱ ✱	987	↑↑	352
	988		351
T T	989		350
↑↑	3011		349
⊞ ⊞	3012		817
L L	3013		815
□ □	830		814
⟨ ⟨	832	∼ ∼	white
	726	∷ ∷	310
⌘ ⌘	727		

Cornfield Table Linen

You Will Need

Antique white 20-count Bellana evenweave (Zweigart code
E3256): 1.4 x 1.4m (1½ x 1½yd) for the tablecloth;
33 x 33cm (13 x 13in) for each napkin

DMC stranded cotton (floss) as listed in chart key,
(1 skein of each colour and 2 skeins of white)

Tapestry needle size 24–26

Matching sewing thread

Stitching the tablecloth

1 Prepare the fabric by neatening the raw edges, pressing
up 1.5cm (⅝in) turnings and stitching the hems in
place. Add decorative hems if you wish.

2 Mark the corner point of each chart 5cm (2in) in from
the corner of the fabric. Follow the charts, working
Design A in two opposite corners and Design C in the
other two corners.

3 Work over two threads of evenweave fabric, from the
corner outwards not the centre point, using two strands
of stranded cotton (floss) for cross stitch and the French
knots in 676, 677 and 613 in the poppy centres.

Work backstitch with
two strands of 986 for
poppy stems, 3011 for
ox-eye daisy stems, 988
for black mustard stems
and 3828 for seed head
stems. Work backstitch
with one strand of 310
for poppy detail, 869
for corn, ox-eye daisy
detail and butterfly
outline, 642 for ox-eye
daisy petals and 3012
for grass stems.

*Design C, worked in two opposite
corners of the tablecloth.*

Stitching the napkins

Prepare the fabric as for the tablecloth. Mark the corner
point of the chart, 2.5cm (1in) in from the corner of the
fabric. Follow the charts, working Design B and Design D
singly on each napkin, twice, to make the set of four. Follow
the tablecloth stitching instructions in step 3.

Cottage Flowers

Flower arranging with abandon is depicted in this lovely picture. A blue and white jug is filled to overflowing with beautiful blooms from a cottage garden – a gorgeous mixture of delphiniums, carnations, chrysanthemums, campanula, sweet pea and gypsophila. A few flowers lie beside the jug, adding to the impression that it has just been filled. The design is straightforward to stitch, using whole and three-quarter cross stitch and backstitch.

Cottage Flowers Picture

Stitch count 200 x 156
Design size 36.5 x 28.5cm (14¼ x 11¼in) approx

You Will Need

Platinum 14-count Aida 57 x 50cm (22¼ x 19¼in)
DMC stranded cotton (floss) as listed in chart key
(1 skein of each colour and 2 skeins each of white and 3755)
Tapestry needle size 24–26

1 Prepare your fabric for work and mark the centre point (see page 98). Work outwards from the centre of the chart overleaf over one block of Aida.

2 Use two strands of stranded cotton (floss) for full and three-quarter cross stitches. Work the backstitch with one strand of 676 for cream carnations, 917 for the pinky-white carnations, white for the pink carnation (shown in light grey on the chart), 642 for chrysanthemum petals and 3051 for the gypsophila (the small white flowers).

3 Once all the stitching is complete, mount and frame your picture (see page 102 for advice).

top left

top right

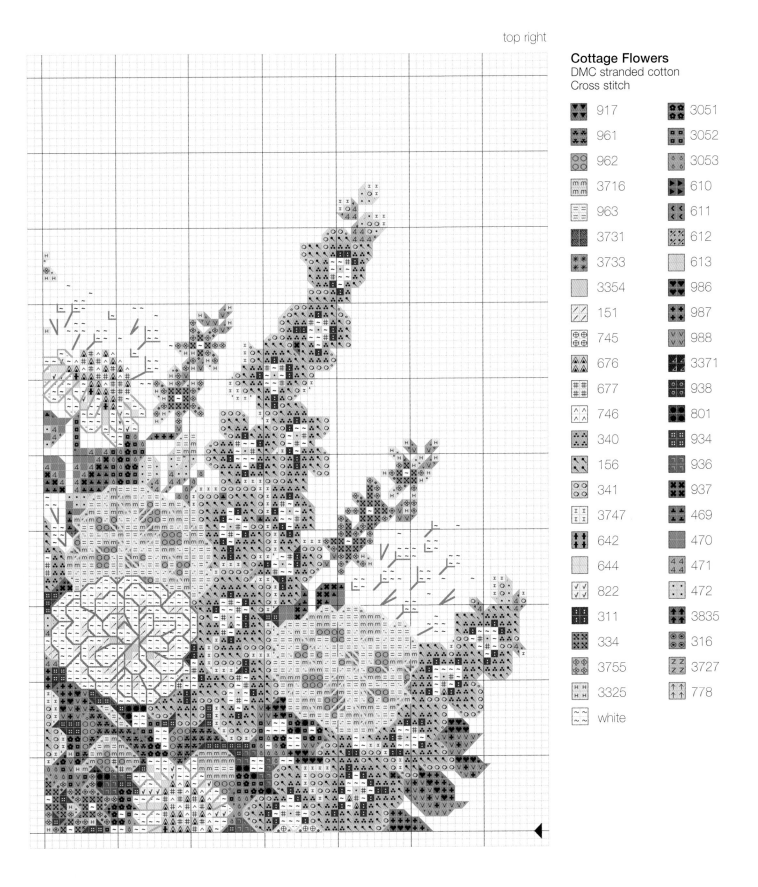

Cottage Flowers
DMC stranded cotton
Cross stitch

917		3051	
961		3052	
962		3053	
3716		610	
963		611	
3731		612	
3733		613	
3354		986	
151		987	
745		988	
676		3371	
677		938	
746		801	
340		934	
156		936	
341		937	
3747		469	
642		470	
644		471	
822		472	
311		3835	
334		316	
3755		3727	
3325		778	
white			

bottom left

bottom right

Cottage Flowers
DMC stranded cotton
Cross stitch

▼▼	917	🌸🌸	3051
✱✱	961	▪▪	3052
OO	962	◊◊	3053
mm	3716	▶▶	610
==	963	<<	611
3731		%%	612
✳✳	3733		613
	3354	♥♥	986
//	151	✛✛	987
⊕⊕	745	VV	988
▲▲	676	44	3371
##	677		938
^^	746		801
∴∴	340		934
↘↘	156		936
OO	341	✖✖	937
II	3747	▲▲	469
++	642		470
	644	44	471
VV	822	∴∴	472
	311	↑↑	3835
✖✖	334	◉◉	316
✿✿	3755	ZZ	3727
HH	3325	↑↑	778
~~	white		

Summer Basket

This fabulously flamboyant design is a mass
of flowers in their full summer glory –
a colourful mixture of petunia, pelargonium,
fuchsia and lobelia creating a wonderful
everlasting hanging basket.
It is shown here stitched as a wall hanging
and mounted on contrasting fabric and
sacking to give it a rustic feel. It would also
brighten any corner stitched as a picture or
cushion on a coloured Aida, perhaps in
cream or sage green. The small spray of
lobelia trailing off the bottom of the Aida
fabric and on to the background fabric is an
attractive and unusual detail, easily added
using waste canvas.

Summer Basket Wall Hanging

Stitch count

190 x 210 excluding inset design

223 x 210 including inset design

Design size

34.5 x 38cm (13½ x 15in) excluding inset design

40.5 x 38cm (16 x 15in) including inset design

Finished size of wall hanging

64 x 67cm (25 x 26in)

You Will Need

Ice-blue 14-count Aida 60 x 56cm (23½ x 22in)

14-count waste canvas 15 x 17cm (6 x 6½in)
for small inset design

DMC stranded cotton (floss) as listed in chart key
(1 skein of each colour)

Tapestry needle size 24–26

Background fabric 60 x 60cm (24 x 24in)

Two pieces of sacking 76 x 76cm (30 x 30in)

Lightweight wadding (batting) 76 x 76cm (30 x 30in)

Matching sewing thread

Wooden pole for hanging 2.5cm (1in) diameter x
76cm (30in) long

Four wooden rings

1 Prepare the Aida for work and mark the centre point
(see page 98). Work outwards from the centre of the
chart on pages 60–63.

2 Use two strands of stranded cotton (floss) for full and
three-quarter cross stitch. Work backstitch with two
strands of 3347 for geranium stems and 919 for fuchsia

stems. Work backstitch with one strand of 347 for fuchsia
stamens and 3346 for lobelia stems. Some of the long,
angled backstitches for the flower stalks could be worked
in long stitch instead.

3 Make up as wall hanging by first trimming the
embroidered fabric down to the desired size. Pin, tack
(baste) and stitch the embroidery centrally on to the
background fabric 1–2cm (½–¾in) in from the edge of
the Aida all round, to allow for a fringe. If, however, you
plan to edge the Aida with braid or cord, then stitch the
embroidery to the background at the edge.

If you wish to stitch the small inset design, continue
with step 4 and onwards: if you wish to omit this detail
then ignore steps 4 and 5 and proceed to steps 6 and 7 to
finish making up the wall hanging.

4 Stitch the small inset design (see detail picture, below)
on the piece of waste canvas: the correct position is
achieved by matching the blue arrow on the small design
with the blue arrow at the bottom of the main design.
Tack (baste) the waste canvas
piece into position with the
blue lines on the canvas
running with the grain
of the background
fabric. Work the cross
stitch and then the
backstitch of the
design over the canvas,
trying to ensure that the
corners of each stitch share
a hole with the previous stitch
in the base fabric. See page 99 for
full details on using waste canvas.

5 When the embroidery is complete, use sharp scissors
to cut away any excess canvas and tweezers to pull out
the vertical canvas threads, followed by the remaining
horizontal threads (see page 99 for diagram). If threads
prove stubborn to remove it may help to dampen them
slightly. Remove tacking (basting).

6 Finish making up the wall hanging by laying the wadding (batting) between the two pieces of sacking, turn the sacking edges inwards to neaten and then pin, tack (baste) and stitch them together. Turn and hem the edges of the background fabric piece and pin, tack (baste) and stitch it centrally on to the sacking. If desired, you could add three decorative borders of running stitch in different colours of six-stranded cotton (floss) on the sacking, as shown in the photograph on page 57.

7 Fray the Aida edges or sew on other decoration of your choice. Finally, sew on four wooden rings at equal distances along the top edge of the sacking and slide them on to the wooden pole to display the wall hanging.

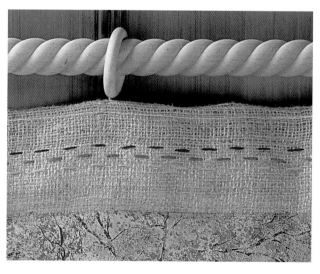

top left

Summer Basket
DMC stranded cotton
Cross stitch

917	351	211	3713	3801	
718	352	347	3778	666	
3608	327	3328	758	321	
817	208	3712	754	815	
349	209	760	948	919	
350	210	761	3770	white	

top right

	831		3013		3345		988		725
	3021		3012		3346		987		796
	3787		3011		3347		986		798
	642		938		3348		3819		799
	644		934		772		581		800
	822		935		989		580		915

bottom left

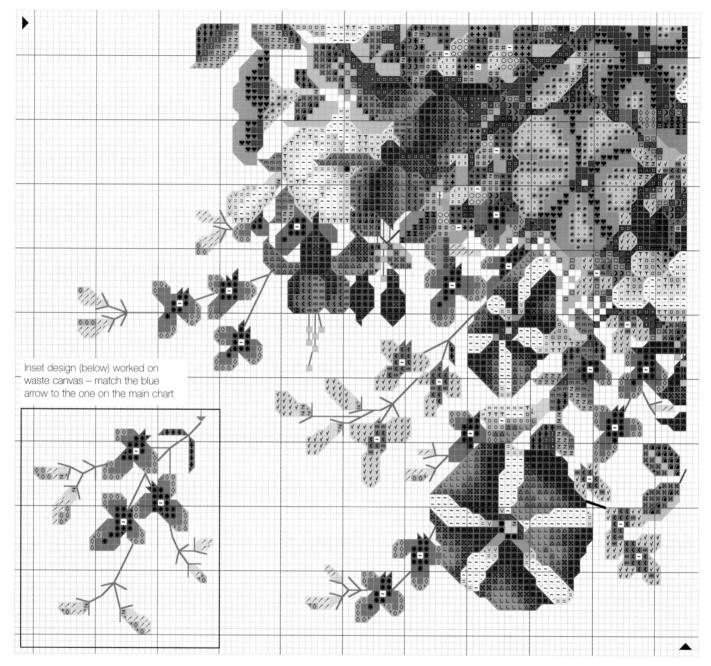

Inset design (below) worked on
waste canvas – match the blue
arrow to the one on the main chart

Summer Basket
DMC stranded cotton
Cross stitch

917	351	211	3713	3801
718	352	347	3778	666
3608	327	3328	758	321
817	208	3712	754	815
349	209	760	948	919
350	210	761	3770	white

bottom right

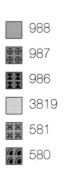

831		3013		3345		988		725
3021		3012		3346		987		796
3787		3011		3347		986		798
642		938		3348		3819		799
644		934		772		581		800
822		935		989		580		915

Clematis Profusion

Clematis – what a flower this is!
Whether you like them dainty and petite or
outrageously flamboyant, they come in
shades that make my artist's mouth water.
They are perfect for covering buildings,
trees, fences or pergolas – always dripping
flowers. This design tries to capture the
profusion with which clematis grow. I've
used the white *Clematis armandii*, which is a
lovely pink in bud, and the vivid mauve and
deep pink *Clematis* 'Sealand Gem'.
The whole design makes a stunning
focal point on a wooden sewing box, while
smaller motifs are used to decorate a useful
needlecase, pin box and pincushion.

Clematis Sewing Box

This lovely box is perfect to display these beautiful clematis. The design uses just full and three-quarter cross stitch and backstitch and would also make a striking picture, the centrepiece for a tablecloth or a cushion.

Stitch count 120 x 120

Design size 19 x 19cm (7½ x 7½in) approx

You Will Need

Cream 16-count Aida 41 x 41cm (16 x 16in)

DMC stranded cotton (floss) as listed in chart key (1 skein of each colour)

Tapestry needle size 24–26

Wooden box 19.5cm (7¾in) square (Market Square, see Suppliers)

1 Prepare your fabric for work and mark the centre point (see page 98). Work outwards from the centre of the chart on pages 68/69.

2 Work over one block of the Aida fabric, using two strands of stranded cotton (floss) for all cross stitch. Work all backstitch using one strand of thread: 934 for the stems and stamens; 223 for the petal details on the pink and white clematis; white for the petal detail on the lilac and pink clematis (the white is shown in grey on the chart for clarity).

3 Once all the stitching is complete, mount your embroidery in the box following the manufacturer's instructions.

Clematis Needlecase

This lovely needlecase will be a pleasure to use, adorned so prettily with a small central section of the main design.

Stitch count 46 x 46

Design size 6.5 x 6.5cm (2½ x 2½in) approx

You Will Need

Sage green 18-count Aida 20 x 20cm (8 x 8in)

DMC stranded cotton (floss) as listed in chart key

Tapestry needle size 24–26

Two 30cm (12in) squares of contrasting colour felt

Matching sewing thread

1 Follow steps 1 and 2 of the sewing box (left) but only stitch the centre section of the design 46 x 46 square. Omit all the backstitch except the stamens in 934. Two rows out from the design add cross stitch borders of one row each of 772, 3346 and 3345.

2 Make up the needlecase by trimming the embroidery to the required size, allowing for a fringed edge if desired. Cut a contrasting piece of coloured felt, 1cm (½in) bigger than the overall size of the design in height and double the width. Cut a second piece of felt slightly smaller than the first. Mark the centre fold line on the width of the larger piece.

3 Place the embroidery centrally on the right side of the large piece of felt, pin, tack, (baste) and stitch into place around the outer edge of the embroidery (allowing for a fringe). Centre the small piece of felt on the opposite side (what will be the inside of the needlecase), pin, tack (baste) and stitch together along the centre fold line. To finish, tease out threads from around the edge of the embroidery to create a fringe.

Pin Box

Stitch count 40 x 32

Design size 5.5 x 4.5cm (2¼ x 1¾in)

Decorate a useful pin box (Framecraft, see Suppliers) using a clematis flower from the main chart. Use a 23 x 21cm (9 x 8in) piece of sage green 18-count Aida and follow the stitching instructions given in steps 1 and 2 of the sewing box. Mount the finished embroidery in the box following the manufacturer's instructions.

Pincushion

Stitch count 41 x 44

Design size 5.75 x 6.25cm (2¼ x 2½in)

Make this pretty pincushion (Framecraft, see Suppliers) by stitching just a small cluster of clematis from the top part of the main design. Work on a 26 x 26cm (10 x 10in) piece of sage green 18-count Aida and follow the stitching instructions in steps 1 and 2 of the sewing box. Mount the finished embroidery in a pincushion following the manufacturer's instructions.

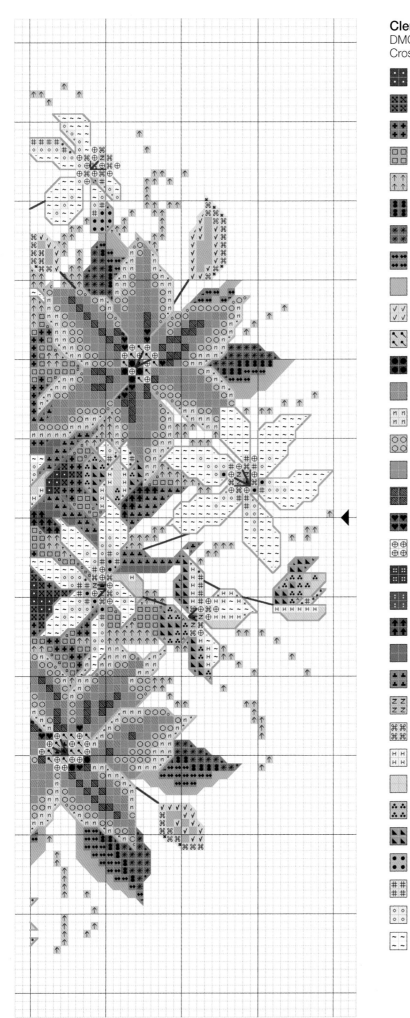

Clematis Profusion
DMC stranded cotton
Cross stitch

Symbol	Code
⚬⚬	3021
✕✕	3787
✚✚	3011
☐☐	3012
↑↑	3013
◼◼	937
✳✳	469
✦✦	470
	471
√√	472
◥◣	402
◼◼	801
	3805
∩∩	153
◯◯	554
	553
◪◪	552
♥♥	550
⊕⊕	3078
⦂⦂	934
⦂⦂	895
▲▲	3345
	3346
▲▲	3347
ᴢᴢ	3348
⌘⌘	772
ʜʜ	225
	224
⁂⁂	152
◣◣	223
●●	169
＃＃	168
∘∘	762
∼∼	white

Flower Garland

This delightful garland features daylilies, Japanese anemones, roses, peonies and dahlias –
all intertwined with ribbon. Using a natural colour fabric creates a subtle over-all effect.
The design is shown as a cushion but could be a stool cover, picture or tablecloth centrepiece.
You could work the anemone centres and gypsophila in French knots for additional texture.

Flower Garland Cushion

Stitch count 181 x 182

Design size 33cm x 33cm (13 x 13in) approx

You Will Need

Natural 14-count Aida 54 x 54cm (21 x 21in)

DMC stranded cotton (floss) as listed in chart key
(1 skein of each colour)

Tapestry needle size 24–26

Fabric for backing and frill 1m (1yd) approx

Cushion pad 38 x 38cm (15 x 15in)

Matching sewing thread

1 Prepare your fabric for work and mark the centre point. Work outwards from the centre of the chart.

2 Work over one block of Aida, using two strands of stranded cotton (floss) for all cross stitch. Although the chart is shown as cross stitch, you could stitch the centres of some of the flowers with French knots instead.

3 Once all the stitching is complete, make up into a frilled cushion – see Workbox page 102.

top left

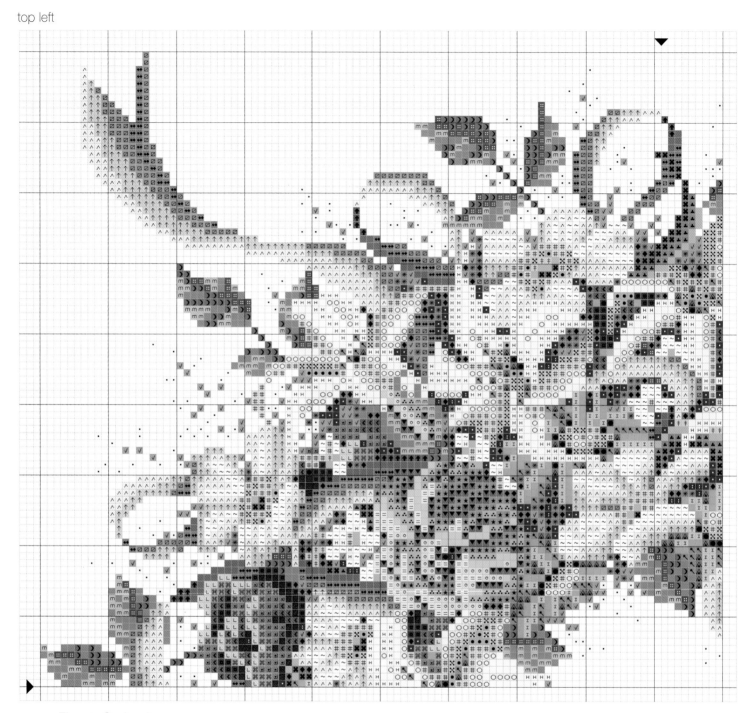

Flower Garland
DMC stranded cotton
Cross stitch

722	817	761	730	224	3053
3825	349	3713	732	225	934
347	350	221	733	741	3345
3328	351	3721	734	742	3346
3712	352	3722	3051	743	3347
760	353	223	3052	744	3348

top right

	745		801
H H H H	3823		938
. . . .	3770	▲ ▲ ▲ ▲	720
~ ~ ~ ~	white		721

bottom left

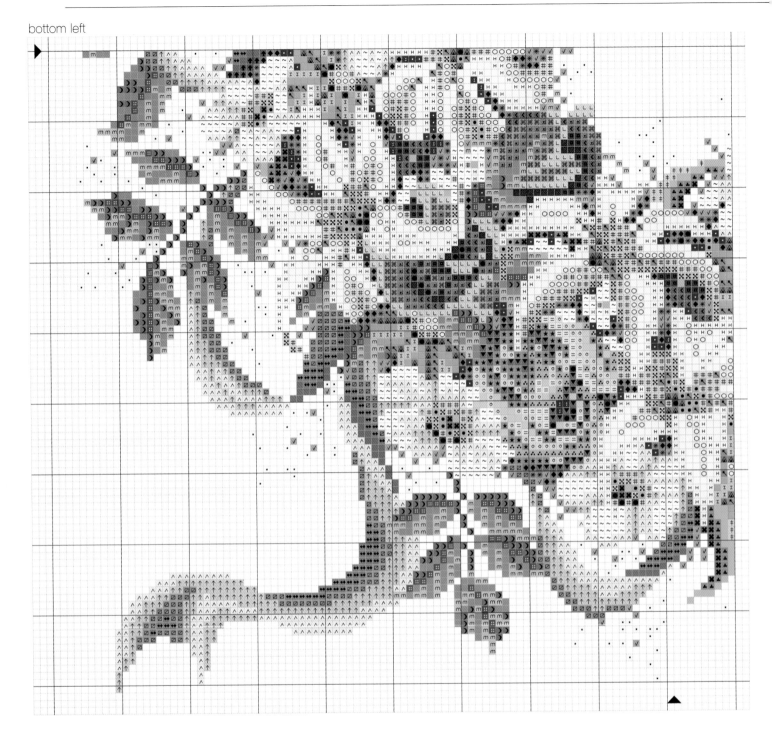

Flower Garland
DMC stranded cotton
Cross stitch

722		817		761		730		224		3053
3825		349		3713		732		225		934
347		350		221		733		741		3345
3328		351		3721		734		742		3346
3712		352		3722		3051		743		3347
760		353		223		3052		744		3348

bottom right

745		801
3823		938
3770		720
white		721

Colourful Cacti

Cacti make excellent subjects for cross stitch and in this chapter I've used two as my inspiration – *Conophytum pearsonii*, sometimes called 'living stones' and a *Mammillaria*, which is often referred to as a pincushion cactus. Both designs show the cacti in flower and surrounded by pebbles, creating bold and colourful statements perfect for modern interiors. The designs are made up in different ways – one framed as a stylish picture and the other decorating a tote bag.

Cactus Picture

This attractive cactus design has a very contemporary look, especially when elegantly framed and mounted. You could also stitch it for a box lid or work individual flowers for cards, coasters or fridge magnets.

Stitch count 110 x 110

Design size 20 x 20cm (7¾ x 7¾in) approx

You Will Need

White 14-count Aida 40 x 40cm (15¾ x 15¾in)

DMC stranded cotton (floss) as listed in chart key (1 skein of each colour)

Tapestry needle size 24–26

1 Prepare your fabric for work and mark the centre point (see page 98). Work outwards from the centre of the chart on page 81. If you prefer, you could use the other cactus design on page 80 as this has the same stitch count.

2 Work over one block of Aida, using two strands of stranded cotton (floss) for all cross stitches.

3 Once all the stitching is complete, mount and frame your picture (see page 102 for advice).

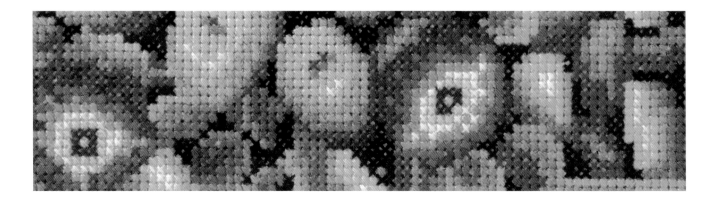

Cactus Bag

A *Mammillaria* cactus design was stitched on waste canvas to create this attractive bag. I chose an interesting fabric with braid detailing for the bag top and handles.

Stitch count 110 x 110

Design size 28 x 28cm (11 x 11in) approx

You Will Need

10-count waste canvas 38 x 38cm (15 x 15in)

DMC stranded cotton (floss) as listed in chart key (1 skein of each colour)

Tapestry needle size 24–26

Medium-weight calico for bag: one piece 69 x 60cm (27 x 23½in) and one piece 48 x 40cm (19 x 15¾in)

Fabric for handles and borders: two 12 x 61cm (4½ x 24in) strips for handles and two 40 x 9cm (15 x 3½in) strips for borders

Matching sewing thread

1 Find the centre point on the large piece of calico by folding the fabric in half both ways. To allow for the border, drop the centre point down 5cm (2in) and mark lightly in pencil. Find the centre point of the waste canvas and lay it over the calico, centre points matching and with the blue lines of the canvas running vertically along the fabric grain. Pin and tack (baste) in place – see using waste canvas on page 99.

2 Stitch the design over the waste canvas, working from the centre outwards, following the chart on page 80 (or the other chart if you prefer). Use two strands of stranded cotton (floss) for all cross stitch.

3 When stitching is complete, remove the tacking (basting), trim away the excess waste canvas close to the cross stitches and then refer to page 99 for removing the canvas. When all canvas threads have been removed, press the embroidery from the wrong side.

4 Make the bag handles by folding the larger strips of fabric in half lengthways, wrong sides facing. Using a 1cm (½in) seam, stitch down each long side then turn right-side out and press with the seam in the centre.

Make the borders for the bag using the smaller fabric strips, turning and pressing a 1cm (½in) seam allowance to the wrong side along one long edge on each piece.

5 Make up the bag by trimming the embroidered fabric to match the smaller calico piece. Turn the top edges of each piece over to the wrong side 1cm (½in), press and stitch down. Place a border piece right side up, with the turned hem at the top, and overlap with the bag front piece by 1cm (½in) at the bottom of the border. Pin, tack (baste) and stitch together. Do the same with the other border piece and the back of the bag. Place the front and back right sides together and then pin, tack (baste) and stitch the sides and bottom using 1cm (½in) seams. Turn right side out.

Sew the handles on to the bag by turning raw edges under and sewing around the edges and then in a cross shape (see detail picture below).

6 To make angled corners for a flat base on the bag, turn the bag inside-out, flatten one base corner to make a right-angled point at the end of the bottom seam (see diagram below). Measure 3.5cm (1½in) down from the end, mark a line across the corner and then sew across the line. Repeat for the other corner.

Stitching an angled corner to create a flat base on the bag.

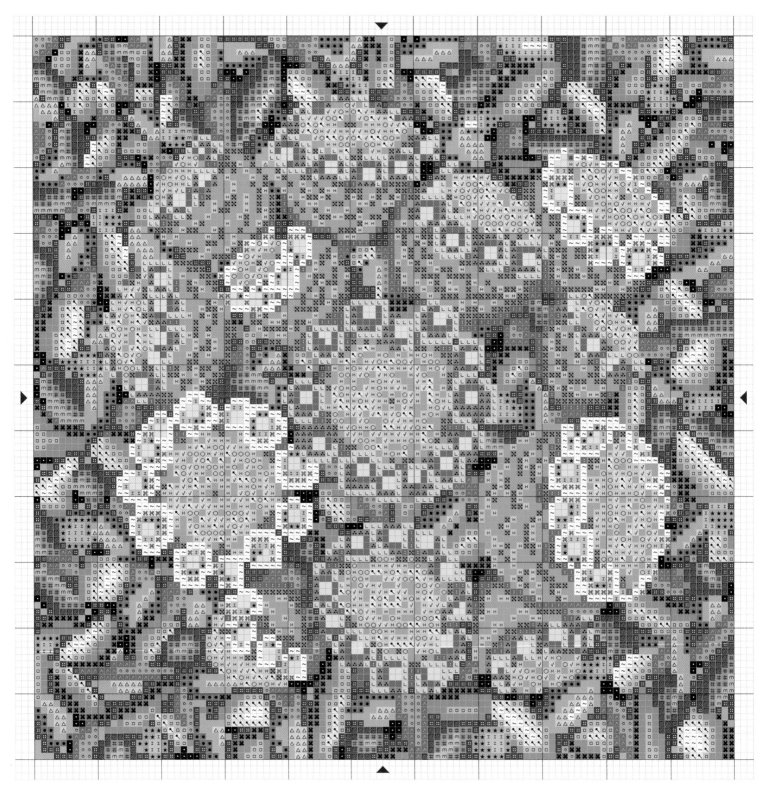

Pincushion Cactus
DMC stranded cotton
Cross stitch

745	841	434	602	3053
420	842	938	604	524
3828	3787	3022	472	white
422	642	3023	936	310
677	437	743	834	
840	436	600	3052	

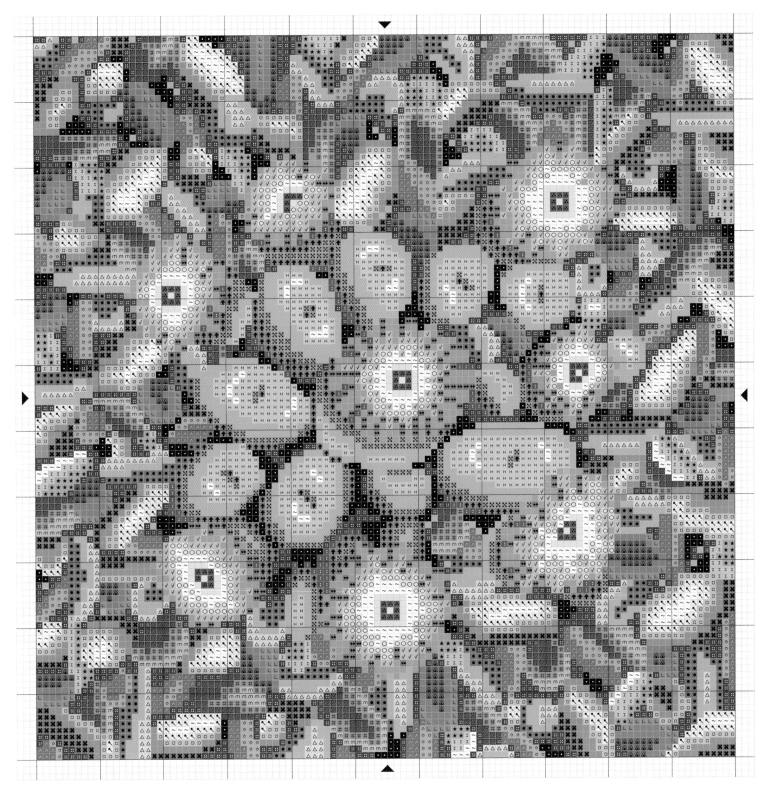

Living Stones Cactus
DMC stranded cotton
Cross stitch

★★ 3022	•• 840	## 436	✖✖ 355	⠇⠇ 500	■• 310	
I I 3023	841	434	743	↑↑ 501		
✖✖ 420	△△ 842	938	OO 3608	✖✖ 502		
3828	^^ 3787	632	√√ 3607	503		
□□ 422	°° 642	3772	718	HH 3813		
◥◥ 677	mm 437	LL 407	✖✖ 917	~~ white		

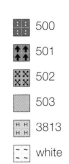

Exotic Trio

Three stunning plants bring a touch of the exotic to this collection of cross-stitched flowers – the iris, named after the Greek goddess of the rainbow, the statuesque crown imperial (*Fritillaria imperialis*) with its topknot of leaves and bell-like flowers and the lovely moth orchid (*Phalaenopsis*). Worked in cross stitch and backstitch, these three pictures would create a striking statement in any interior with their tall, elegant shapes and contrasting forms.

Iris, Fritillary and Orchid Pictures

Stitch count (for each flower) 210 x 80
Design size (for each flower) 38 x 14.5cm (15 x 5¾in)

You Will Need (for each flower)

Dark fawn 28-count Zweigart Cashel linen (code 346)
60 x 35cm (23 x 14in)

DMC stranded cotton (floss) as listed in chart key
(1 skein of each colour)

Tapestry needle size 24–26

1 Prepare your fabric for work and mark the centre point (see page 98). Work outwards from the centre of the charts provided on pages 84–89.

2 Work over two threads of linen, using two strands of stranded cotton (floss) for all full and three-quarter cross stitch. Work backstitch using one strand as follows: white for purple iris petal edges (shown in grey on the chart for clarity), 3041 for dusty-pink iris petal edges, 791 for iris flower centre details, white for orchid petal edges (shown in black on chart), 3727 for orchid stamens and 920 for fritillary petal edges.

3 Once all the stitching is complete, mount and frame your picture (see page 102 for advice).

top half

bottom half

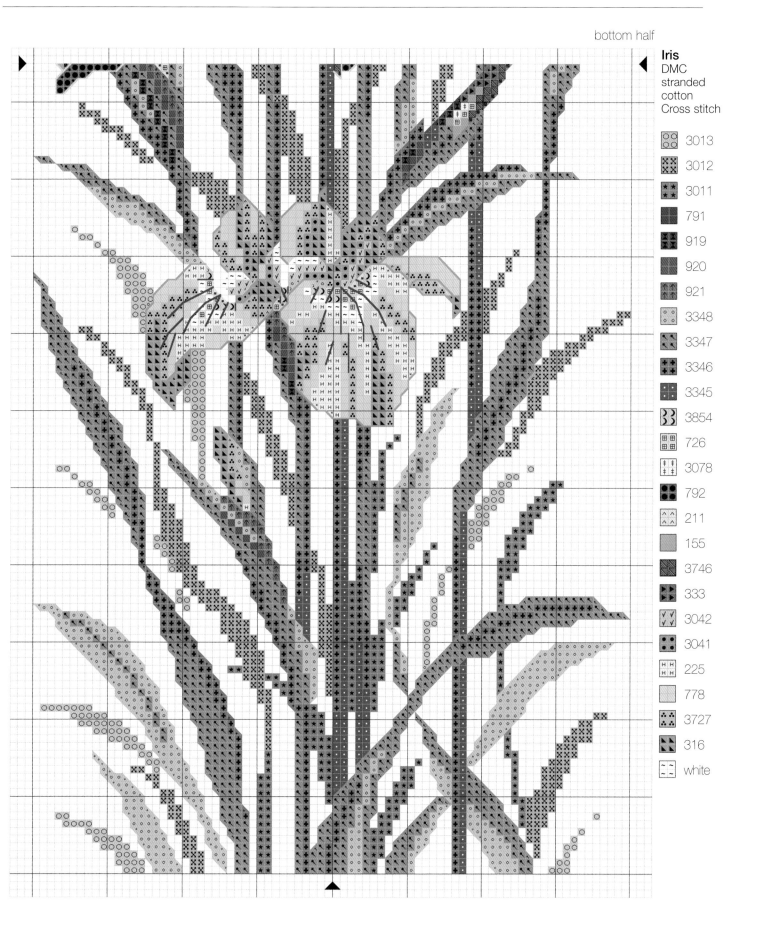

Iris
DMC
stranded
cotton
Cross stitch

3013
3012
3011
791
919
920
921
3348
3347
3346
3345
3854
726
3078
792
211
155
3746
333
3042
3041
225
778
3727
316
white

top half

bottom half

Fritillary
DMC
stranded
cotton
Cross stitch

3013
3012
3011
3371
779
934
936
937
469
470
471
472
938
918
920
677
746
951
3856
722
721
720

top half

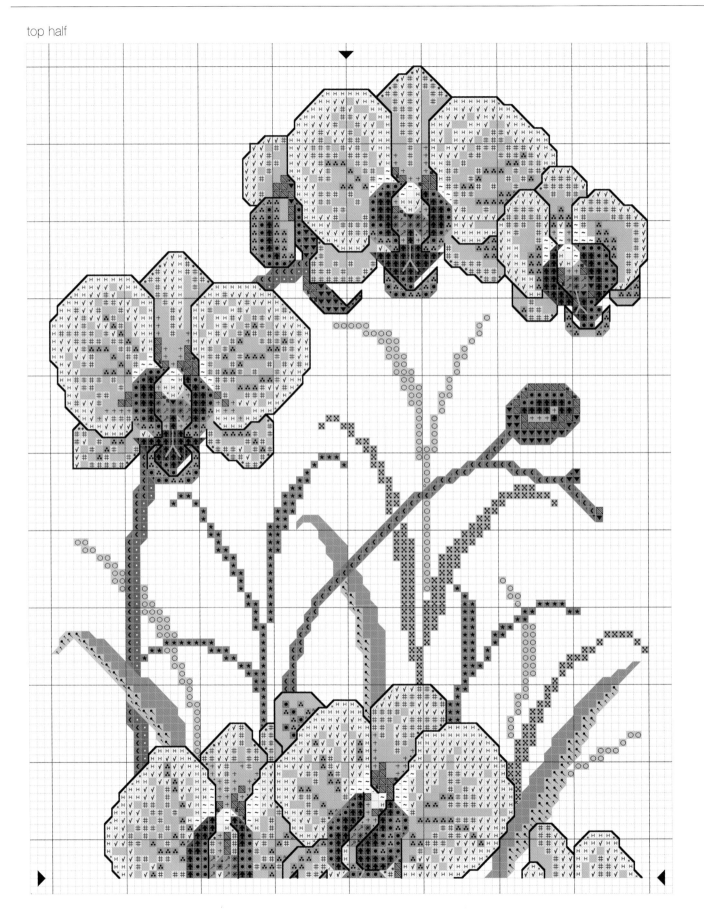

bottom half

Orchid
DMC
stranded
cotton
Cross stitch

3013	
3012	
3011	
3346	
3347	
3348	
3078	
319	
367	
315	
316	
3727	
720	
721	
915	
917	
718	
3607	
3608	
3609	
818	
white	

Floral Portraits

This final collection of flowers contains many of my favourites. The three smaller designs – pansy, dahlia and echinacea (coneflower) – have been stitched within the trellis pattern of squares on a wonderful Afghan throw. The three larger designs – water lily, marigold and sunflower – have been used to create coasters, described on page 92, and for a plant poke, cards and a notelet holder, shown on page 93.

All of the designs are very versatile – try using them on different fabric counts to create different sized motifs, on waste canvas to decorate clothing or on Aida bands to embellish household linen. Refer to the charts for stitch counts and design sizes.

Floral Throw

Pansies, dahlias and echinacea (coneflower) have been stitched within the squares of an Afghan fabric to make a beautiful throw. To create more texture, work French knots in the flower centres instead of cross stitch. The finished size of the throw is 100 x 60cm (39 x 24in).

You Will Need

White 18-count Afghan fabric 117 x 74cm (46 x 29in)

DMC stranded cotton (floss) as listed in chart key
(1 skein of each colour;
2 skeins of 321, 552, 553, 602, 605, 606, 666, 816;
3 skeins of white, 550, 554)

Tapestry needle size 24–26

Matching sewing thread

1 Iron the Afghan fabric if necessary and then stitch several rows of machine stitches close to the outer edge on the outside squares of the fabric to create the fringing later. Mark the centre point of each square on the Afghan fabric.

2 Follow the charts on pages 94–95, using three strands of stranded cotton (floss) for all cross stitch and working over two threads. Add a border of three lines of cross stitches at the outer edge to finish – I used DMC 550, 554 and 602.

3 When stitching is complete, tease out threads at the outer edges of the fabric for a fringe. The machine stitches will prevent the fabric from fraying too far.

Floral Coasters

Two plastic coasters (from Framecraft, see Suppliers) are perfect for displaying a dahlia and pansy portrait, worked on 18 x 18cm (7 x 7in) pieces of cream 16-count Aida. Prepare your fabric, mark the centre point and then follow the charts on pages 94 and 95, using two strands of stranded cotton (floss) for all cross stitch. Refer to the manufacturer's instructions for mounting in the coaster.

Plant Poke

This cheerful plant poke features the sunflower design but you could use any of the other floral portraits.

You Will Need

White 11-count Aida 26 x 26cm (10 x 10in)

DMC stranded cotton (floss) as listed in chart key

Tapestry needle size 24–26

Green felt (or your choice of colour) 15 x 15cm (6 x 6in)

Matching sewing thread

Garden stick

1 Prepare your fabric for work and mark the centre point (see page 98). Follow the sunflower chart on page 96, using three strands of stranded cotton (floss) for all cross stitch. Trim the finished embroidery to within one block of the design all round.

2 Pin the embroidery face up on to the piece of felt and trim the felt to match the embroidery. Tack (baste) and stitch the two pieces together around the edge, leaving a small gap at the bottom. Push a garden stick up through the gap between the two layers so it is held firmly in place.

Greetings Cards

Use the floral portraits to create a series of pretty greetings cards. Here, the water lily and marigold have been worked on 15 x 21cm (6 x 8in) pieces of 18-count Aida in pewter and Christmas green and mounted in cream cards with 9.5 x 14cm (3¾ x 5½in) apertures (from Framecraft, see Suppliers). Prepare your fabric and mark the centre point. Follow the charts on pages 95 and 96, using two strands of stranded cotton (floss) for all cross stitch. Mount the embroidery in the card as described on page 102.

Notelet Case

This handy notelet case (from Framecraft, see Suppliers) has two sunflowers and a marigold worked on a 46 x 21cm (18 x 8in) piece of cream 18-count Aida. Follow the charts on page 96, using two strands of stranded cotton (floss) for all cross stitch and working the designs in a row – use the template provided with the case. Refer to the manufacturer's instructions for mounting the completed embroideries in the case.

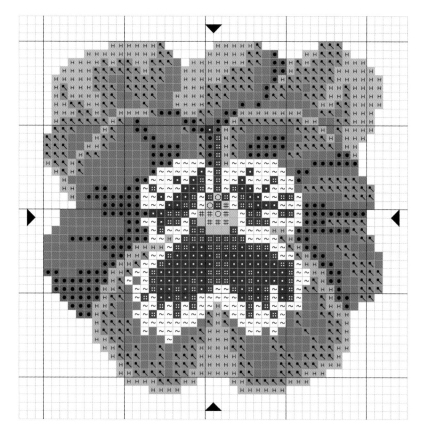

Pansy
DMC stranded cotton
Cross stitch

- 725
- 472
- 726
- 939
- 154
- 550
- 552
- 553
- 554
- white

Stitch count 42 x 42
Design size (on 14-count) 8 x 8cm (3 x 3in)

Echinacea
DMC stranded cotton
Cross stitch

- 600
- 601
- 602
- 603
- 604
- 605
- 938
- 918
- 919
- 920
- 921
- 922
- white

Stitch count 42 x 42
Design size (on 14-count) 8 x 8cm (3 x 3in)

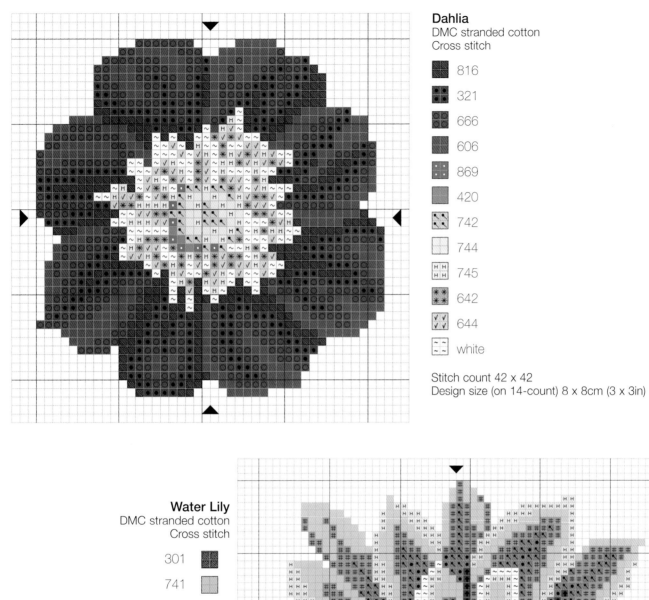

Dahlia
DMC stranded cotton
Cross stitch

■	816
■	321
■	666
■	606
■	869
■	420
■	742
■	744
H H / H H	745
* * / * *	642
√ √ / √ √	644
~ ~ / ~ ~	white

Stitch count 42 x 42
Design size (on 14-count) 8 x 8cm (3 x 3in)

Water Lily
DMC stranded cotton
Cross stitch

301	■
741	■
742	^ ^ / ^ ^
3803	■
3687	■
961	■
962	# # / # #
3716	■
963	H H / H H
white	~ ~ / ~ ~

Stitch count 55 x 55
Design size (on 14-count) 10 x 10cm (4 x 4in)

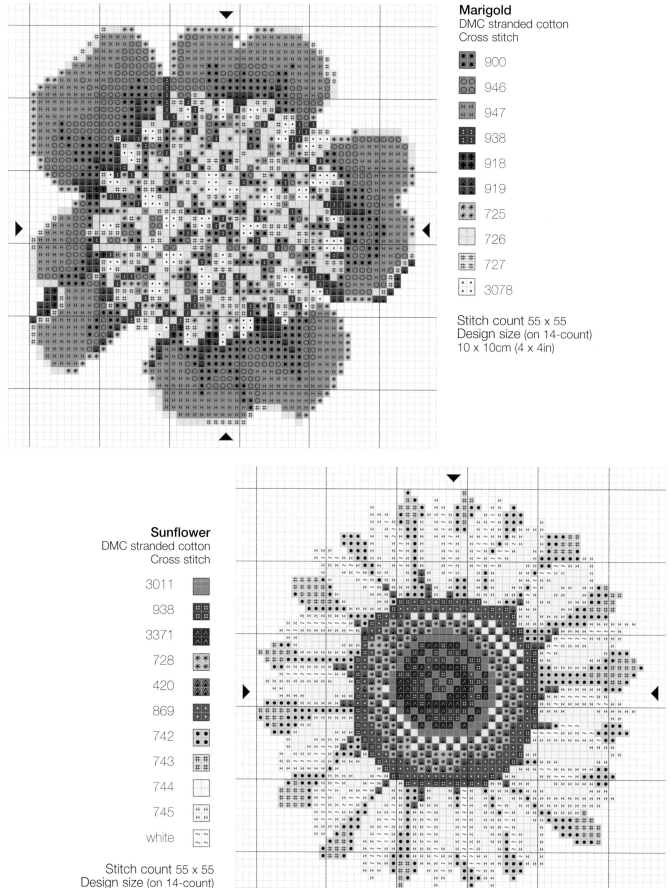

Marigold
DMC stranded cotton
Cross stitch

900
946
947
938
918
919
725
726
727
3078

Stitch count 55 x 55
Design size (on 14-count)
10 x 10cm (4 x 4in)

Sunflower
DMC stranded cotton
Cross stitch

3011
938
3371
728
420
869
742
743
744
745
white

Stitch count 55 x 55
Design size (on 14-count)
10 x 10cm (4 x 4in)

Workbox

This chapter gives you all the information you will need to produce perfect cross stitch embroidery and successfully recreate the projects in this book. There is advice on materials and equipment, embroidery techniques, stitches and making up methods.

Materials and Equipment

This short section describes the basic materials and equipment you will need.

Fabrics

Most of the designs in this book have been worked on Aida fabric which is stitched over one block. The main size used is 14 blocks or threads to 1in (2.5cm), often called 14-count. Some designs use an evenweave fabric such as linen which should be worked over two threads. The same design stitched on fabrics of different counts will work up as different sizes. The larger the count, the more threads per 1in (2.5cm), therefore the smaller the finished design, and vice versa. Each project lists the type of fabric used, giving the thread count and fabric name. All DMC threads and fabrics are available from good needle-work shops (see Suppliers for details).

Threads

If you want your designs to look the same as those shown in the photo-graphs, you need to use the colours and threads listed for each project. I've used DMC stranded cotton (floss) but there is an Anchor conversion table on page 106. Some projects can be stitched with tapestry wool (yarn) instead.

It is best to keep threads tidy and manageable with thread organizers and project cards. Cut the threads to equal lengths and loop them into project cards with the thread shade code and colour key symbol noted at the side. This will prevent threads becoming tangled and codes being lost.

Stranded cotton (floss)

This is the most widely used embroidery thread and is available in hundreds of colours, including silver and gold metallic. It is made from six strands twisted together to form a thick thread, which can be used whole or split into thinner strands. The type of fabric used will determine how many strands of thread you use: most of the designs in this book use two strands for cross stitch and one for backstitch.

Tapestry wool (yarn)

DMC wool is a matt, hairy yarn made from 100 per cent wool fibres twisted together to make a thick single thread which cannot be split. Designs using tapestry wool are usually worked on a canvas using one or two strands.

A wide selection of colours is available, with shades tending to be slightly duller than for stranded cotton. There are conversion lists for colour matching from stranded cotton to tapestry yarn – ask at your needlework shop.

Needles

Stitch your designs using a tapestry needle which has a large eye and a blunt end to prevent damage to the fabric. Choose a size of needle that will slide easily through the fabric holes without distorting or enlarging them. If using beads to enhance a design you will need to use a beading needle, which is thinner and longer.

Scissors

You will need sharp embroidery scissors for cutting threads and good dressmaking scissors for cutting fabric.

Embroidery Frames

Your work will be much easier to handle and stitches will be kept flat and smooth if you mount your fabric on an embroidery hoop or frame, which will accommodate the whole design. Bind the outer ring of a hoop with a white bias tape to prevent it from marking the fabric. This will also keep the fabric taut and prevent it from slipping whilst you are working.

Basic Techniques

The following techniques and tips will help you attain a professional finish by showing you how to prepare for work, work the stitches and care for your embroidery.

Preparing Fabric

Spending a little time preparing your embroidery fabric for work is a good idea, helping to avoid mistakes and produce superior finished results.

Fabric sizes Make sure you are using the correct size of fabric by checking the stitch count (the number of stitches across the height and width of the design) and design size given with each project. Each project gives the finished size of a design when worked on the recommended fabric, together with the amount of fabric needed. The overall fabric size should be at least 8–10cm (3–4in) larger than the finished size of the design to allow for turnings or seam allowances when mounting the work or making it up. To prevent fabric from fraying, machine stitch around the edges or bind with tape. Measurements are given in metric with imperial equivalent in brackets. Always use either metric or imperial – do not mix the two.

Centre point Starting your stitching from the centre point of the fabric ensures you will have enough fabric all round the design. To find the centre point, tack (baste) a row of stitches horizontally and vertically from the centre of each side of the fabric. These lines correspond to the arrows at the side of each chart and will cross at the centre point.

Using Charts

All the designs in this book use DMC embroidery fabrics and stranded cotton (floss). The colours and symbols shown on the chart keys correspond to DMC shade codes. Each coloured square on the chart represents one complete cross stitch and some squares also have a symbol. The colours and symbols correspond to those in the key beside each chart. A small triangle in a corner of a grid square represents a three-quarter cross stitch. French knots are shown by a coloured dot – the project instructions specify what thread shade to use. Solid coloured lines indicate backstitch or long stitch – refer to the project instructions for details. The optional use of beads on a design will be in the instructions and will also specify which colours they replace.

Small black arrows at the side of a chart indicate the centre, and by lining these up you can find the centre point. Some of the charts are spread over four pages with the key repeated on each double page. Work systematically so you read the chart accurately and avoid mistakes. Constantly check your progress against the chart and count the stitches as you go. If your sight is poor you may find it helpful to enlarge a chart on a colour photocopier.

Using Tapestry Canvas

Many of the projects can also be stitched on canvas with tapestry wool (yarn) – perfect for more hard-wearing items such as doorstops, rugs and wall hangings. Ask at your local needle-work shop for a conversion list to change stranded cotton (floss) colours to wool (yarn). Remember that when working on canvas you will also need a complementary background wool colour to fill in the canvas area around the design.

There is a range of canvas available in craft shops, from lighter weights used for embroidery to heavier canvas used for rugs. Canvas is basically of two types – tapestry and embroidery, as mono and interlock. Tapestry and embroidery canvases are ideal if the design has whole and three-quarter cross stitches or half and quarter cross stitches. Mono and interlock are ideal if the design has all whole cross stitch or half cross stitch.

When altering the count a design is stitched on, remember the design size will change so you need to work out carefully what size canvas is required. The count will tell you how many stitches there are to every 2.5cm (1in). All of the projects have design sizes and stitch counts listed. Simply divide the stitch count by the fabric or canvas count to calculate the size of the design area, without any allowance. Always be generous with allowances, as you can trim the excess off. When working on canvas, add at least 13–15cm (5–6in) allowance all the way around a design.

Using Waste Canvas

Waste canvas allows you to work a design on textured fabrics, household items and clothing. It is available in various counts and is used just like Aida. It has blue lines that mark off every five blocks making it easier to count stitches.

To use waste canvas, cut a piece of canvas at least 5cm (2in) larger than the design you wish to stitch. Lay the canvas over the base fabric so the blue lines run vertically along the fabric grain. Pin and tack (baste) in place and mark the centre (Fig 1). Stitch the design over the waste canvas following the project instructions for the cross stitch. When working, try to ensure that the corners of each stitch share a

hole with the previous stitch in the base fabric as this will give a much neater finished effect.

When the stitching is complete, remove tacking (basting) threads, and trim away excess waste canvas close to the cross stitches. Use tweezers to carefully pull out the vertical threads of the waste canvas – the remaining horizontal threads can then be easily removed (Fig 2). If the canvas threads prove stubborn to remove it may help to slightly dampen them.

When all the canvas threads have been completely removed, press the embroidery from the wrong side, then add any backstitches, French knots or beads to complete your design.

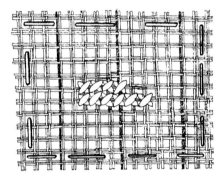

Fig 1 Tacking (basting) a piece of waste canvas into position.

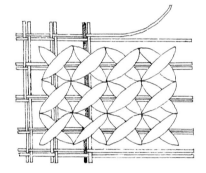

Fig 2 Removing waste canvas threads once the cross stitch is completed.

This detail picture shows the finished effect once the waste canvas threads are removed.

Adding Beads

Designs can be greatly enhanced by replacing a single thread colour or a whole section of full cross stitches with beads.

Use a thin beading needle to sew on beads with matching thread, starting with the needle on the right side of the fabric. Thread the bead over the needle on to the thread and attach to the fabric with a half cross stitch. All stitches should run in the same direction so the beads lie in neat rows.

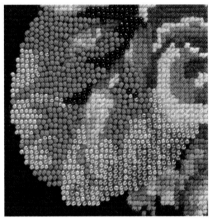

Choose from the wonderful range of beads available from your craft shop and also mail-order companies.

Washing and Pressing Embroidery

If your work has become grubby during stitching, gently hand wash in warm water using a mild liquid detergent. Do not rub or wring the embroidery. If necessary, use a soft nail brush to gently remove any stubborn marks. Rinse in clean water and then place the damp fabric on a clean white towel and leave to dry on a flat surface. Do not iron directly on your embroidery as this will flatten the stitches and spoil the finished effect. Lay the work face down on a thick, clean white towel, cover with a clean fine cloth and press carefully with a medium iron, taking extra care with any beads or metallic threads.

The Stitches

This section shows how to work the stitches used in the book. When following these instructions, note that stitching is over one block of Aida or two threads of evenweave.

Starting and Finishing Thread

To start off your first length of thread, make a knot at one end and push the needle through to the back of the fabric, about 3cm (1¼in) from your starting point, leaving the knot on the right side. Stitch towards the knot, securing the thread at the back of the fabric as you go (Fig 3). When the thread is secure, cut off the knot.

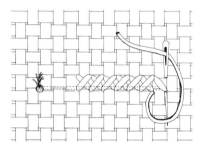

Fig 3 Starting to stitch.

To finish off a thread or start new threads, simply weave the thread into the back of several stitches (Fig 4).

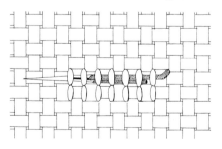

Fig 4 Finishing off a thread.

Backstitch

Backstitch is indicated on the charts by a solid coloured line. It is worked around areas of completed cross stitches to add definition, or on top of stitches to add detail.

To work backstitch (Fig 5), pull the needle through the hole in the fabric at 1 and back through at 2. For the next stitch, pull the needle through at 3, then push to the back at 1, and repeat the process to make the next stitch. If working backstitch on an evenweave fabric, work each backstitch over two threads.

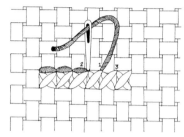

Fig 5 Working backstitch.

Bullion Knots

These knots are wonderful for adding three-dimensional texture to designs.

Follow Fig 6, right, bringing the needle up at 1 and down at 2, but do not pull the thread through (a). Stab the needle up at 1 again but bring it only halfway through the material (b). Holding the needle from below, wind the thread around it until the number of twists equals the distance between 1 and 2 (c). Holding the top of the needle and thread firmly with thumb and finger, draw the needle through, loosening the coil of threads with your hand as you do so, to allow the needle to pass through freely (d). Place the needle against the end of the twist, at the same time pulling the thread until the knot lies flat on the material. If any bumps appear in the knot, flatten these by stroking them beneath the twist with the needle, at the same time pulling the thread (e). Put needle into the fabric, close to the end of the twist, and pull through firmly (f).

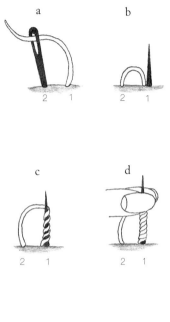

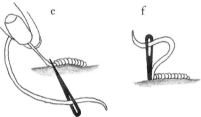

Fig 6 Working a bullion knot.

The completed bullion knots add realistic, three-dimensional texture.

Cross Stitch

Each coloured square on a chart represents one complete cross stitch. Cross stitch is worked in two easy stages. Start by working one diagonal stitch over one block of Aida (Fig 7) or two threads of evenweave (Fig 8), then work a second diagonal stitch over the first stitch, but in the opposite direction to form a cross.

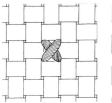

Fig 7 A cross stitch on Aida fabric.   *Fig 8 A cross stitch on evenweave fabric.*

Cross stitches can be worked in rows if you have a large area to cover. Work a row of half cross stitches in one direction and then back in the opposite direction with the diagonal stitches to complete each cross. The upper stitches of all the crosses should lie in the same direction to produce a neat effect (Fig 9).

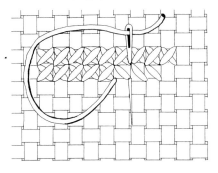

Fig 9 Working cross stitch in rows.

Quarter Cross Stitch

If you chose to work a design on a double mesh canvas using wool (yarn), a quarter cross stitch should be used instead of a three-quarter cross stitch. To work, start at one corner of the canvas mesh and work in the same direction as any half stitches but insert the needle at the corner of the square.

Half Cross Stitch

This stitch is also used if you chose to work a design on canvas in tapestry wool (yarn), replacing whole cross stitches with half stitches. A half cross stitch is simply one half of a cross stitch, with the diagonal facing the same way as the upper stitches of each complete cross stitch (Fig 10).

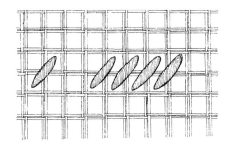

Fig 10 Working half cross stitch.

Three-quarter Cross Stitch

A small coloured triangle taking up half a chart square represents a three-quarter cross stitch. Forming fractional stitches is less accurate on Aida than on evenweave because the centre of the Aida block needs to be pierced.

Work the first half of a cross stitch in the normal way, then work the second diagonal stitch in the opposite corner but insert the needle at the centre of the cross, forming three-quarters of the complete stitch (Fig 11). A square showing two smaller coloured triangles in opposite corners indicates that two three-quarter cross stitches will have to be worked back to back, sharing holes.

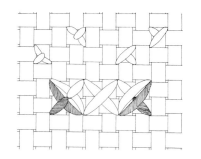

Fig 11 Working three-quarter cross stitch.

French Knots

These are small knots used for details, indicated on charts by coloured dots.

To work a French knot, bring the needle through to the front of the fabric, just above the point you want the stitch placed. Wind the thread once around the needle and, holding the twisted thread firmly, insert the needle a little away from its starting position (Fig 12). Two tips for working French knots: never rush them and never go back into the same point where your thread came up or your knot will pull through to the back.

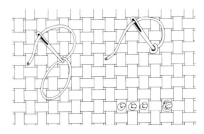

Fig 12 Working French knots.

Long Stitch

These are used to work some flower stems and are indicated on charts by a straight coloured line – refer to the instructions for the colour. Work long stitches on top of cross stitches.

To work long stitch, pull the needle through the fabric at the point indicated on the chart and push it through at the other end shown on the chart, to make a long, straight stitch on top of the fabric. Repeat for the next stitch, carrying the thread across the back of the fabric to the next starting point (Fig 13).

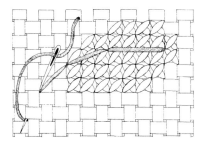

Fig 13 Working long stitch.

Making Up

This section describes how to make up the embroideries as illustrated, although the designs are simple to adapt and use in many different ways, with suggestions given throughout the book. When making up any item, a 1.5cm (⁵⁄₈in) seam allowance has been used unless otherwise stated.

Mounting and Framing

It really is best to take larger pictures to a professional framer, who will be able to stretch the fabric correctly and cut any surrounding mounts accurately. If, however, you prefer to mount and frame yourself you will need a mitre box for cutting mitred edges on frames, some panel pins, a suitable saw, some hardboard (or thick card) and mount board. When choosing mount board and a frame, it is best to take your finished work with you, to get an idea of what the end result will be.

Mount your embroidery on to thin hardboard or card and fasten by lacing it around the card or by stapling. Decide on the frame size you require and carefully cut your frame pieces to the correct size, then panel pin them together. Using a mount cutter or a craft or Stanley knife, cut your mount board to the required depth. Place the mount board into the frame, then the embroidery. Finally, cut hardboard to size for the backing and wedge in with metal clips or tape in place.

Ready-Made Items

Many of the projects in the book can be displayed in ready-made items such as cards, coasters, trinket boxes, pincushions and footstools. There are various manufacturers supplying such items (see Suppliers). Smaller pieces of embroidery can be backed with an iron-on interfacing (such as Vilene) to firm up the fabric and prevent wrinkling, and then be mounted in the item following the manufacturer's instructions.

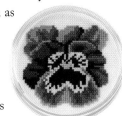

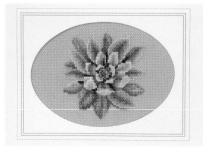

When mounting work in cards, trim the embroidery so it is slightly larger than the card aperture and use double-sided tape inside the card around the aperture, pressing the embroidery on to the tape. The Framecraft cards I use already have this tape in place.

Frilled Cushion

These instructions are for a 38 x 38cm (15 x 15in) cushion with a gathered, frilled edge but the principles can be applied to any size. You will need a cushion pad, matching sewing thread and sufficient fabric for backing and making a frill.

Carefully cut away the excess embroidery fabric leaving the cushion front as a square with a 1.5cm (⁵⁄₈in) seam allowance. Now cut two pieces of cotton fabric 25.5 x 38cm (10 x 15in) for the cushion back. Take each of these rectangles and hem along one long edge.

To make the frill, cut enough 12cm (4³⁄₄in) wide strips along the length of the fabric to give a finished length of about 3.75m (4yd). With right sides facing, stitch the fabric strips together along the short edges to form a circle (Fig 14). Press seams open. Fold the strips in half so the long edges meet, enclosing the raw edges of the short seams, and then press.

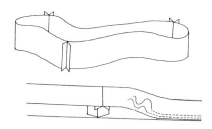

Fig 14 Making a cushion frill.

Run two lines of gathering threads along the raw edges of the frill fabric, then pull up the thread until the frill is the right length, distributing gathers evenly. With the embroidered fabric facing upwards, place the frill around the outer edge of the cushion front, so raw edges face outwards. Distribute the gathers evenly, then pin, tack (baste) and machine stitch in place.

Lay the embroidered fabric face up on a flat surface. With right sides down, lay the two rectangles of the cushion back on top of the front so all raw edges match and hemmed edges overlap at the centre. Pin, tack (baste) and then machine stitch along the stitching line and through all layers of fabric. Neaten the raw edges, then turn the cover through to the right side and insert a cushion pad.

Braid-Edged Cushion with Tassels

This type of cushion makes an elegant statement and could be used to display many of the designs. A pincushion could also be made following the same principles. You will need a cushion pad, matching sewing thread, sufficient fabric for backing and enough thick furnishing braid to go around your cushion. Follow the instructions for making the frilled cushion, left, but omit the frill.

After making the cushion cover, turn it through to the right side. Measure the length of the cushion edges, then cut lengths of braid to the same measurements, adding 10cm (4in) to each length. Hand stitch the braid along each edge, leaving equal lengths extending at each end.

To make a simple tassel, pinch together the two lengths of braid extending from each corner, then use matching sewing thread to bind them tightly together. Secure the sewing thread with a knot, then fray the braid to make a tassel (Fig 15).

Fig 15 Creating a simple tassel.

Stitching Tips

✓ Steam press your embroidery fabric before stitching to remove any stubborn creases.

✓ Mount fabric on to an embroidery frame or hoop to keep stitches smooth and flat.

✓ For a neat appearance, work cross stitches with the top diagonals facing in the same direction.

✓ Thread up lengths of several colours of stranded cotton (floss) into needles, and arrange these at the side of your work by shade code or by key reference.

✓ Work the designs from the centre outwards, or split them into workable sections such as quarters. On larger designs, first work the main subject and then complete the background and surrounding designs.

✓ When taking threads across the back of a design, weave the thread through the back of existing stitches to avoid any ugly lines showing through on the right side.

✓ Use short lengths of thread, about 30cm (12in), to reduce the likelihood of knotting and tangling.

✓ Check your work constantly against the chart to avoid making counting mistakes.

✓ For smooth embroidery without lumps, avoid using knots at the back, and cut off any excess threads as short as possible.

✓ Keep your work clean by packing it away in its own clean plastic bag to prevent any accidents.

Suppliers

If you should require any further information about products, catalogues, price lists or local stockists from any of the suppliers mentioned, contact them direct by post or phone. Remember to always include a stamped, addressed envelope. If contacting them by phone, they will be able to tell you if there is any charge for the catalogue or price lists.

DMC Creative World Ltd
Pullman Road, Wigston,
Leicestershire LE18 2DY, UK
tel: (0116) 281 1040
www.dmc.com
For threads, embroidery fabrics and beads used in the book, and for the name and address of your nearest DMC and Zweigart stockist

DMC threads are supplied in the USA by:
The DMC Corporation,
South Hackensack Ave, Port Kearny,
Building 10A, South Kearny,
NJ 07032-4688, USA
www.dmc-usa.com

Zweigart fabric is supplied in the USA by:
Joan Toggitt Ltd, 2 River View Drive,
Somerset, NJ 08873-1139, USA
email: info@zweigart.com
www.zweigart.com

Framecraft Miniatures Ltd
Unit 3, Isis House, Lindon Road,
Brownhills, West Midlands
WS8 7BW, UK
tel: 01543 360842
www.framecraft.com
For ready-made items for embroidery, including cards, trinket pots, coasters, notelet cases, pincushions and pin boxes

Framecraft products are also supplied worldwide by:
Anne Brinkley Designs Inc
761 Palmer Avenue, Holmdel,
NJ 97733, USA

Gay Bowles Sales Inc
PO Box 1060, Janesville,
WI 53547, USA

Ireland Needlecraft Pty Ltd
4, 2–4 Keppel Drive, Hallam,
Vic 3803, Australia

Market Square (Warminster) Ltd
Wing Farm, Longbridge Deverill,
Warminster, Wiltshire BA12 7DD, UK
tel: 01985 841042
Suppliers of footstools and needlework boxes

Vilene products were used on some projects in the book. Iron-on interfacings are available in major department stores and haberdashery shops (notions departments).

© Chris Mayhead

About the Author
Jayne Netley Mayhew is a renowned wildlife artist and cross stitch designer. She takes her inspiration from nature and her designs are detailed and varied, from frogs and dolphins to lions and panthers. Her work features regularly in needlecraft and needlework magazines and is also available from Janlynn Kits and DMC.

Acknowledgments
A very special thank you to my husband Ian, for all his support, help and patient understanding while I worked on this book. A thank you also goes to Lorraine, who has helped me make up the items in this book – a lifelong friend who's always there. Another huge thank you to John Parkes of Outpost Trading, who, as usual without a moan, had to rush my framing through at the last moment. Thank you also to Jean and Don Halstead for letting me include the recreation of their grandmother's footstool, which was originally created in the mid to late 1800s. A big thank you to Cara Ackerman at DMC and Sarah Carlton-Gray at Framecraft Miniatures Ltd for their support.

Thank you also to the following people for their contributions and help with getting this book published: Doreen Montgomery for her support, invaluable as always. Cheryl Brown for keeping me producing new books. Linda Clements for her invaluable help perfecting my text. Ali Myer and Lisa Forrester for the beautiful book design. Many thanks also to Kim Sayer and Karl Adamson for the wonderful photography.

Index

DMC–Anchor Conversion Table

This conversion chart is only a guide as exact colour comparisons cannot always be made between different thread manufacturers.

DMC	ANCHOR	DMC	ANCHOR	DMC	ANCHOR	DMC	ANCHOR	DMC	ANCHOR
White	2	472	253	779	380	962	75	3787	904
Ecru	387	498	1005	783	307	963	23	3801	1098
150	59	500	683	791	178	970	925	3803	69
151	73	501	878	792	941	976	1001	3805	62
152	969	502	877	793	176	986	246	3807	122
153	95	503	876	794	175	987	244	3813	875
154	873	524	858	796	133	988	243	3819	278
155	1030	550	101	798	146	989	242	3820	306
156	118	552	99	799	145	3011	856	3821	305
168	274	553	98	800	144	3012	855	3822	295
169	849	554	95	801	359	3013	853	3823	386
208	110	563	208	814	45	3021	905	3825	323
209	109	580	924	815	44	3022	8581	3826	1049
210	108	581	281	816	43	3023	899	3828	373
211	342	600	59	817	13	3033	387	3834	100
221	897	601	63	818	23	3041	871	3835	98
223	895	602	57	819	271	3042	870	3852	306
224	893	603	62	822	390	3046	887	3854	313
225	1026	604	55	823	152	3051	845	3856	347
301	1049	605	1094	830	277	3052	844		
309	42	606	334	831	277	3053	843		
310	403	610	889	832	907	3072	397		
311	148	611	898	834	874	3078	292		
315	1019	612	832	840	1084	3325	129		
316	1017	613	831	841	1082	3326	36		
317	400	632	936	842	1080	3328	1024		
319	1044	642	392	869	375	3345	268		
320	215	644	391	890	218	3346	267		
321	47	648	900	891	35	3347	266		
322	978	666	46	892	33	3348	264		
326	59	676	891	893	27	3350	77		
327	101	677	361	894	26	3354	74		
333	119	718	88	895	1044	3371	382		
334	977	720	326	898	380	3607	87		
335	40	721	324	899	38	3608	86		
340	118	722	323	900	333	3609	85		
341	117	725	305	902	897	3687	68		
347	1025	726	295	915	1029	3688	75		
349	13	727	293	917	89	3689	49		
350	11	728	305	918	341	3706	33		
351	10	730	845	919	340	3712	1023		
352	9	732	281	920	1004	3713	1020		
353	8	733	280	921	1003	3716	25		
355	1014	734	279	922	1003	3721	896		
367	216	741	304	926	850	3722	1027		
368	214	742	303	927	849	3726	1018		
369	1043	743	302	928	274	3727	1016		
402	1047	744	301	934	862	3731	76		
407	914	745	300	935	861	3733	75		
413	236	746	275	936	846	3746	1030		
420	374	754	1012	937	268	3747	120		
422	372	758	9575	938	381	3752	1032		
434	310	760	1022	939	152	3753	1031		
436	363	761	1021	946	332	3755	140		
437	362	762	234	947	330	3770	1009		
469	267	772	259	948	1011	3772	1007		
470	266	776	24	951	1010	3778	1013		
471	265	778	968	961	76	3782	388		